The Book of Bizarre Football

The Book of Bizarre Football

Freaky forwards, strange strikers, dodgy defenders and other soccer sensations from 1900–2000

Graham Sharpe

To Kenilworth Road and Lower Mead

First published in Great Britain in 2000 by Robson Books,
10 Blenheim Court, Brewery Road, London N7 9NT

A member of the Chrysalis Group plc

British Library Cataloguing in Publication Data
A catalogue record for this title is available from the British Library

ISBN 1 86105 291 X

Typeset by SX Composing DTP, Rayleigh, Essex
Printed in Great Britain by Creative Print & Design (Wales), Ebbw Vale

CONTENTS

INTRODUCTION

There are those who would allege that I have been involved in a fair share of bizarre happenings on and around football pitches in North West London over the past forty-nine years.

It is, I admit, true that I used to wear gloss-painted orange football boots – but you couldn't buy coloured boots then; and I must confess to wearing tassels instead of sock tie-ups – but that was in tribute to my hero, the great Muhammad Ali, who used to have such attachments on his boxing boots. And, yes, I would invariably take part in matches with a handkerchief protruding from the waistband of my shorts – but I never did discover how everyone else blew their nose during a game.

My qualifications for writing a book on the bizarre and eccentric side of football include my very name – well, the real footballer with whom I share it was from North of the Border, spelt it differently, and scored fewer goals than I did during his career – albeit his were notched at slightly higher level; and then there are the four decades of supporting two of the country's less glamorous clubs – Luton Town and Wealdstone, the latter of which was the first club of both Stuart Pearce and Vinnie Jones, the latter of which, bizarrely enough, was the only semi-pro footballer I ever heard of who was actively encouraged to play Sunday football by his boss, on the grounds that that was the only way he was likely to be able to guarantee himself ninety minutes of playing during a weekend. I was an ever so slightly temperamental player for the likes of Wealdstone Athletic; Hatch End; Alveston and Parkfield – once being, unjustly, sent off for 'teasing' and once booked for answering a mobile phone call whilst attacking down the right wing. It is also true that I was once, unjustly, red-carded by the man at whose wedding I served as best man, Graham 'Whistler' Brown. As a director of Wealdstone – whilst writing this, at any rate – I am facing a charge of bringing the game into disrepute for daring to speak my mind in print in the club programme. As a manager I took Hatch End to four successive Sunday League titles but narrowly failed in my bid to succeed Graham Taylor as England manager when my application to the then FA top man Graham Kelly, who was well aware of my day-job in the world of bookmaking, resulted in a response suggesting that I shouldn't bet on getting the job.

I have always believed that the crucial feature of football matches is that almost every single one contains some kind of incident which is remarkable, newsworthy, or just plain daft. These are the yarns I have endeavoured to assemble within these pages – in an effort to make you raise an eyebrow, scratch your head and want to share these priceless nuggets of information instantly with a friend at school, at work, in the pub or club, or even in the grandstand or on the terraces of your favourite ground.

I make no claims that I have produced anything other than an entertaining, sideways look at the game, but I enjoyed putting it together and am optimistic that you will discover herein many eccentricities and unorthodoxies of which you would otherwise have remained in total ignorance, and that I will have convinced you that, as the splendid mangler of the English language, Gianluca Vialli, once observed: "It's an old, funny game . . ."

Graham Sharpe

ADVERTISEMENTS

Leeds, England and former Newcastle hard man David Batty was not best pleased when he was pictured wearing stockings and suspenders, plus stiletto heels and a Newcastle shirt, in a controversial image produced by Channel 5 to advertise their coverage of the club's European match against Partizan Belgrade in 1998.

Seeking to draw attention to a campaign on behalf of the Mines Advisory Group, their agency produced a series of controversial adverts in 1998, one of which read: 'What's The Cheapest Way To Clear A Minefield?' – '22 Kids And A Football.'

An advertisement hoarding for a solicitor at Bradford's Valley Parade ground read 'Kama Sutra: We'll defend you in difficult positions.'

In 1995 Brentford were claiming the world's biggest

Bob Thompson, who played for Chelsea in 1915, is the only **one**-eyed player to appear in the FA Cup Final.

advertisement for the slogan 'Next Time . . . Fly KLM' emblazoned on their main stand roof. And EasyJet painted 'We've Got the Balls' on the roof of their stand, which is under the Heathrow flight path, during 1999.

Irked at being abused by Reading fans, Bristol City defender Gerard Lavin kicked the ball hard at an advertising board during a Second Division game in August 1999, only to miss and hit Reading supporter Mark Stevens, 37, breaking his wrist.

Ian Wright . . . Chicken Tonight
David Ginola . . . L'Oreal shampoo, Laguna cars
David Beckham . . . Brylcreem
Alan Shearer . . . McDonalds
John Hartson . . . Hair replacement treatment

AGE CONCERN

In January 1999, 82-year-old Dr Hugh Symons was still turning out for London Hospital Old Boys – having scored a hat-trick at the age of 79.

Keeper Dick Pym, of England, Bolton and Exeter, was the oldest lived international when he died aged 95 in 1988.

Tom Clarke, 79 at the time, claimed to be the world's oldest active ref in June 1999 when he was supervising four matches a week in the City of Manchester League.

Alberto Cuero received rave reviews for his performance for

After scoring **two** goals in ten games, Derby's Argentinian striker Esteban Fuertes was deported in November 1999 for allegedly travelling on a forged passport.

Ecuador in the 1999 South American Under-17 Championships – before his father revealed that he was actually 20.

Non-league soccer fan Sam Phillips, a supporter of Ledbury Town, was banned from their ground in 1980 for allegedly assaulting a referee. Not an unusual story in itself – except that Sam was over 80 years old.

AIR

Italian club Fiorentina launched a new line in the club shop during 1999 – cans of air from the Artemio Franchi Stadium, labelled as Air of the Terraces, Essence of Victory and Dressing-room Atmosphere.

ALCOHOL

The first known example of the booze getting the better of a star footballer came in 1898, when Scottish centre-half Jamie Cowan, an Aston Villa player, turned in a mysterious performance against England at Parkhead as the Scots went down 3–1. Failing to make his tackles and going on a series of eccentric dribbles with the ball, Cowan was blamed by the crowd and a number of his team-mates for the defeat. The Scottish FA later held an enquiry at which the player was accused of being under the influence and although not officially censured, he never played for Scotland again.

Liverpool legend Billy Liddell, who played over 400 games for the Anfield club and won 28 Scottish caps, was such a strict abstainer from alcohol that when Liverpool won the League championship in 1947 'he refused to take the ritual sip of champagne from the cup'. So, when he broke the record of

Fainting after his vasectomy, Northern League ref Russell Tiffin hit his head and was hospitalised for **three** days with concussion.

429 League games for Liverpool, the club naturally presented him with a 'cocktail cabinet loaded with all kinds of liquor'.

Scottish brewer Douglas Ross came up with a winner for Euro 2000 – an ale created specially to celebrate his country's qualification for the final stages of the tournament. But when they missed out to England the Stirling man had to swallow his pride and rename the beer 'England Euro 2000 Ale'.

Newly appointed Chelsea boss Gianluca Vialli, in his first match since replacing the fired Ruud Gullit, gave his players a glass of champagne each before they went out and beat Arsenal 3–1 to reach the Coca-Cola Cup final on 18 February 1998. Commented striker Mark Hughes: 'It was cheap stuff – but we didn't spit it out.' The FA's thoughts on alcoholically hyped-up players went unrecorded!

Four Russian officials appointed to referee the September 1999 UEFA Cup tie between Hapoel Haifa and Club Bruges were sacked after arriving at Tel Aviv drunk. They attempted to fondle women police officers and broke into an impromptu song and dance routine on arrival at Ben-Gurion airport. Sergei Kosiano, Sarvon Martinov, Sergei Husseinov and Pavel Ginzburg were then taken to a restaurant where they 'kissed the hands of waitresses and insisted on filling their glasses with whisky' before rushing into the street where they began directing the traffic. Four Romanian officials were quickly flown in to take charge of the game, which Haifa won 3–1.

A 1993 Romanian League third division play-off game had to be halted when one side, Chirnogeni, 21–0 down, could field only six players – as all the rest of the squad were still drunk

The North Wales Sunday League match between Maesgeirchen and Amlwch in November 1999 was abandoned after all **four** of the club's match-balls were deposited into the nearby Menai Straits by ill-aimed shots.

from celebrating a team-mate's wedding the night before.

ANARCHISTS

A group of Italian anarchists dedicated to 'causing panic in the sanctuaries of power' adopted the collective identity of former Watford and AC Milan player Luther Blissett, to hide their true identities. In March 1997 four members of the group appeared in court accused of failing to pay train fares and all answered 'Luther Blissett' when asked for their names. In 1999 the group published a 650-page book under the authorship of 'Luther Blissett'. In a statement the group said they had chosen Blissett because he was 'a nice Afro-Caribbean guy who had problems with the Italian way of playing football and became a target of racist jokes. The Luther Blissett project is a way of taking revenge on stupidity.'

Blissett, back at Watford, commented: 'I am not pleased, but what can you do about it?'

ANTHEM

Warbling the US national anthem during the opening ceremony for the 1994 World Cup, John Secada was at one second singing in full view of a TV audience of one billion people – the next he vanished, having fallen through a hole in the stage. Trouper that he is, Secada carried on singing regardless, with only his head on view, before being carted off to hospital with a dislocated shoulder.

ARC AT THIS

Graeme Murty of Reading was asked in the club programme who he'd most like to meet: 'Joan of Arc – the one who rode naked through the streets.'

At the age of just **five** months, Oliver Newton became the youngest person ever to visit every League ground in England.

ARMS

Six months after losing both arms in a 44,000-volt shock at the power sub-station where he was working, 40-year-old Robert Cooke returned to manage Welsh League side Pontardawe for the 1999–2000 season. 'I'm not too sensitive. The lads call me armless, ask me to lend them a hand and tell me to keep my fingers crossed for the season,' he said.

Andie Wilson of Chelsea was a popular, successful inside-forward despite losing the use of one arm during the First World War, which couldn't have helped when he later went on to become an international bowler.

Arsenal's Steve Morrow broke his arm after Tony Adams hoisted him on to his shoulders and then dropped him during celebrations after their victory over Sheffield Wednesday in the 1993 Coca-Cola Cup final.

Times columnist Danny Baker revealed his nomination for 'the harshest refereeing decision of all time' in an article in November 1998. He related the story of a player, identified only as Richard, who plays in the Bristol area despite having lost an arm in an accident at work. During the course of a match he was defending in his own box when the ball struck 'the hanging cuff portion of his vacant shirt sleeve', whereupon the referee awarded a penalty against him. 'After several minutes of outraged protestations, the penalised player sloshes the ref with his existing arm and is properly sent off.'

Alf Bond, who refereed the 1956 FA Cup final, had only one arm.

Geoff Hurst was the last player to score **six** goals in a League match – doing so in West Ham's 8–0 First Division win against Sunderland on 19 October 1968.

When Wrexham won the Welsh Cup in 1893 they did it under the captaincy of one-armed Arthur Lea.

ATTACK

First Division linesman Edward Martin was knocked unconscious by a spectator during a 1998 match at Portsmouth's Fratton Park ground against Sheffield United.

In February 1992 referee Roger Wiseman was attacked during a game between Birmingham and Stoke and, after a delay, the game was completed in an empty stadium.

Ref Rodger Gifford was attacked on the pitch at Ewood Park in February 1995 as Blackburn played Leeds.

Forward Scott McGleish was attacked by a spectator after scoring at Brighton for Orient in March 1997.

AUCTION

An auction was held at the Hotel Metropole in Leeds in 1919 – of all the players of Leeds City, who had been expelled from the League for failing to permit their books to be inspected.

Scottish side Queen's Park conceded their first goal in **seven** years on 16 January 1875.

BABY

Darlington claimed to be keeping tabs on an up-and-coming player in February 1999. It might be a while before he makes the first team, though, as Ben Wright was only 21 months old at the time.

Fans Paul and Celestine Taylor registered their first baby for Reading supporters' club 28 weeks into his mother's pregnancy – supplying a scan photo of the foetus to appear on his membership card. The unborn, unnamed child due to be born only that October, was listed in August 1999 as Baby Taylor.

When officials at Devon club Seaton Town spotted the footballing ability of George Harwood, they signed him up on a 13-year contract to prevent rivals from poaching him – even though he was just 18 months old at the time in January 1999.

After losing 2–1 at home to Valencia, who finished the game with just **eight** players, in December 1999, Atletico Madrid's president Jesus Gil offered season ticket holders a complete refund.

Chelsea midfielder Dennis Wise's girlfriend Claire Dunn became a millennimum when she gave birth to Henry 88 minutes into the new century. Henry later achieved further fame when appearing on the Wembley pitch with dad following Chelsea's 2000 FA Cup victory.

BALLS

Forty million footballs are sold throughout the world each year.

The match ball burst during both the 1946 and 1947 FA Cup finals.

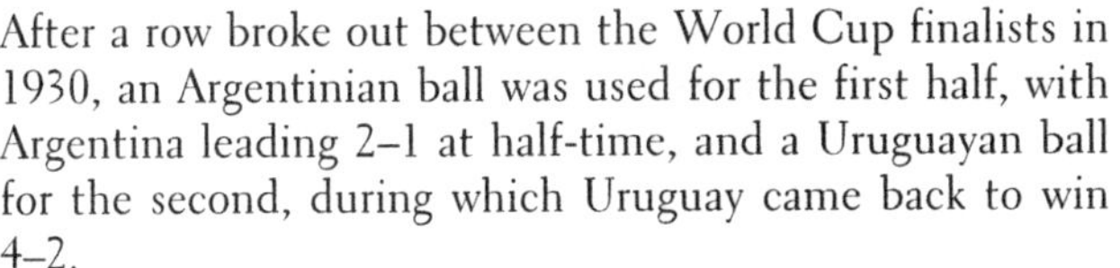

After a row broke out between the World Cup finalists in 1930, an Argentinian ball was used for the first half, with Argentina leading 2–1 at half-time, and a Uruguayan ball for the second, during which Uruguay came back to win 4–2.

Brazilian ace Ronaldo teamed up with a new girlfriend in August 1999 – one who could boast a footballing claim to fame which the superstar could not match. Twenty-year-old Milene Domingues set a world record for 'keepy-uppy' in 1995, scoring 55,187 touches of the ball in 9 hrs 6 mins.

The *Peterborough Evening Telegraph* abandoned its Spot The Ball competition in the first week of February 1995 because it left the ball in the photograph.

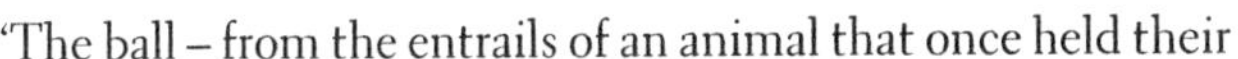

'The ball – from the entrails of an animal that once held their

Watford's Steve Palmer wore the number **nine** shirt against Fulham on 2 May to complete a unique record of wearing every shirt number from 1 to 14 during the 1997–98 season.

own supernatural mystery – is in itself symbolic. It means more than it is, an object of fecundity related to all that is fecund.' Percy M. Young in his *History of British Football*, 1968.

Keeper Fabio Costa of Brazilian side Vitoria held on to the ball for ten minutes after letting in a penalty which cut his side's lead against Atletico Mineiro to 2–1 with time running out. His refusal to hand over the ball led to a mass punch-up in which two players were sent off. When the ref finally persuaded him to surrender the ball, the game carried on. Just four minutes of additional time were added and the score in the September 1999 game remained unchanged.

Trevor Senior of Reading scored a hat-trick at Cardiff in September 1995 but was refused permission to keep the ball. 'If he wants to give us £40 then he can have it,' declared Cardiff boss Alan Durban.

Most of us have played football with someone who has believed their ownership of the ball gives them complete autonomy over the interpretation of the rules of the game. Perhaps that was what was behind the story which appeared in a 1920 edition of the *Belfast Morning News*: 'Irish FA Protests and Appeals Committee: Arising out of the match played last Saturday, a report was made that a player of Dunmurry would not give up the ball at the conclusion of the match. It was decided if the ball be not returned before Monday 22nd inst, the club stand suspended.'

BANNED

Playing for Manchester United at Crystal Palace, Eric

Lieutenant Edmund Creswell of Royal Engineers was the first man ever injured in an FA Cup final, breaking his collar bone after **ten** minutes of the first final in 1872.

Cantona aimed a kung-fu kick at Palace fan Matthew Simmons, who had abused him verbally from the crowd. Cantona was sentenced to 120 hours of community service, fined by the FA and banned from playing for eight months.

When Argentinian coach Daniel Passarella took over the squad for the 1998 World Cup he banned long hair, earrings and homosexuals.

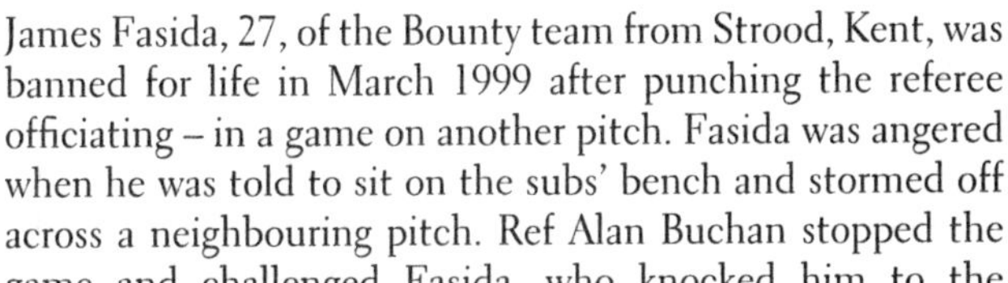

James Fasida, 27, of the Bounty team from Strood, Kent, was banned for life in March 1999 after punching the referee officiating – in a game on another pitch. Fasida was angered when he was told to sit on the subs' bench and stormed off across a neighbouring pitch. Ref Alan Buchan stopped the game and challenged Fasida, who knocked him to the ground and punched a spectator.

BED

In 1969 a Huddersfield fan watched his heroes play against Blackpool from pitchside – whilst lying in bed. Nineteen-year-old David Tagg had been bedridden for eight years, but the club arranged for a removal van to collect him and his hospital bed and transfer them to a corner-flag location from where he watched Huddersfield win 2–0.

BEEF

Coventry's £4 million Moroccan star Moustapha Hadji played for two months with a slice of British beefsteak strapped to his right foot after bruising his instep at the start of the 1999–2000 season.

Brighton midfielder Charlie Oatway, named by his QPR-supporting parents after their 1973 side, has **eleven** christian names – none of which is Charlie.

BENEFIT

Walter Cartwright made 257 appearances for Manchester United between 1895 and 1904, but his benefit match was not a great success, earning him £1 6s – which he spent on a night out in Crewe. In 1999 Sir Alex Ferguson made a reported £1 million tax free from his benefit game.

BETTING

The earliest reference to betting on football matches surfaces for the first FA Cup final, in which 4/7 shots the Royal Engineers became the game's first beaten odds-on favourites – with a man called, ironically enough, Betts, scoring the only goal of the game for the Wanderers. Football betting today is a hugely popular pastime with over £1,000 million gambled on it each year. Between the two points there have been some remarkable stories.

In 1890 a Sheffield magistrate, Edwin Richmond, pushed through a council resolution instructing the chief librarian to delete all betting news contained in papers kept by the local libraries.

Officials and players were banned from betting on matches in 1892.

By 1895 the National Anti-Gambling League were out to prosecute publishing companies for accepting stake money on newspaper football betting coupons.

In 1902 the FA attempted the impossible – banning

'I spent **twelve** years as a player at Tottenham and when my contract ends at Wimbledon I will have been there 12 years. I'm a bit of a one-club man.' Joe Kinnear.

everyone who attended a football match from betting on its outcome.

A 1907 survey purported to show that up to 250,000 football fixed-odds betting coupons were collected in a single week in Liverpool.

Three men caught distributing football betting coupons outside Villa Park on match day were arrested and offered a choice of a £1 fine or 14 days inside in 1909.

By 1910 J.C. Clegg, a senior FA official, was warning: 'If ever betting got a firm foothold, the game as we know it would be done forever.'

The spectre of match-fixing reared its head in the 1911–12 season and a book, *The Story of the Football League*, referring to that season, declared: 'At this time the game began to be the object of increased activity amongst betting agents who did not hesitate to get into contact with players and give rise to suspicions regarding the bona-fides of certain games.'

The *Morning Post* estimated in 1913 that two million football coupons were being circulated nationally on a weekly basis.

The Times was demanding the 'suppression of the football bookmakers who prey on the gullible public' in November 1922 – and in the same year Crystal Palace were ordered to remove from their ground a hoarding advertising football betting.

The official crowd at Old Trafford for a game between Stockport County and Leicester City in May 1921 was **thirteen**.

They weren't the first, but in 1923 what would become the Littlewoods Pools company launched their first coupon, distributing 4,000 of them and getting back 35 entries totalling £4 7s 6d (£4.37½), of which £2.60 was returned in winnings.

During the 1935–36 season the Football League made a farcical effort to scupper football betting by introducing a system whereby fixtures would be arranged on a week-by-week basis, with clubs being sworn to secrecy so that pools promoters would be prevented from preparing coupons in time for distribution. This ill-fated, badly thought-out idea lasted just a couple of weeks – fixtures were leaked to the press, while attendances dropped as spectators were thoroughly bewildered by the whole affair.

A private member's Bill to make pools betting illegal was crushed by 287 votes to 24 in 1936.

William Hill launched his first fixed-odds football coupon in 1939 and took £6.92½.

Anticipating the Lottery's good causes by many years, Unity Pools, an umbrella grouping of the established companies used during the Second World War, earmarked a part of their takings for charity.

Just before Pools Betting Duty was introduced in 1948 there were 231 pools firms. By 1951 only 42 remained.

In 1953 former MP and author A.P. Herbert summed up the

Johann Cruyff always wore a number **fourteen** shirt.

'crazy state of Britain's betting laws' in his book, *Pools Pilot*: 'Messrs Z do football betting at fixed odds only. They have a large office in London, and another, it is said, in Scotland. If you send them a bet in London you must not send the money with it – that would be "ready money" betting which (off the course) is illegal. You may send it next week, for then it will be credit betting, which is all right.

'Exactly the same law applies to Bonny Scotland. But, to put it mildly, it does not carry the same weight in those far parts. Our friend and neighbour, Mr Blanket, like many other Londoners, sends his money with his bet to the Scottish office of Messrs Z every week. Mr Blanket believes he is lawfully doing cash betting in Scotland.

'Mr Blanket's bet on the Obvious Eight, with its humble shilling, is carried to Bonny Scotland by train. But it is not then hurried to Messrs Z's great Scottish office; for Messrs Z have no great Scottish office, though they have a small one. The sack of wagers is now transferred to an aircraft and conveyed back to London. Mr Blanket's little ready-money bet is deemed to have acquired legality by its brief visit to Scotland. This, we think is about the funniest thing that happens in this island, and it happens every week.'

A year later the Pools Betting Act made it legal for stakes to be sent in with current coupons.

In 1957 Nellie McGrail of Stockport became the first £200,000 pools winner, receiving her Littlewoods cheque from Norman Wisdom.

In March 1960 John Moores, Littlewoods founder, became a director of Everton FC, but had to resign his pools and bookmaking directorships to do so.

Sheffield Wednesday have been around long enough to have received a trophy from Oliver Cromwell – the Cromwell Cup was handed over on **fifteen** February 1868 when they beat Garrick in a competition named after and presented by the manager of the Alexandra Theatre.

A fixed-odds betting price war broke out amongst bookies, who were offering odds of up to 60/1 for predicting just three draws. In October 1962 one week produced 26 draws in total. The biggest fixed-odds company, William Hill, paid out £1,312,810 to winners.

A 1976 Gallup survey found that 37 per cent of the adult population bet on football pools – 89 per cent of those on a weekly basis.

Ron Noades, then Crystal Palace chairman, was amongst the leaders of a group of 75 clubs on both sides of the border who launched their own pools competition at the start of the 1985–86 season. It collapsed within three months, with reported losses to clubs of over £1 million.

Nursing sister Margaret Francis and ten colleagues from Roundway Psychiatric Hospital in Wiltshire became the first million-pound pools winners in 1986 – their winning selections had been made by patients.

At the beginning of the 1987–88 season Luton Town became the first club to permit a bookmaker to operate inside their ground. Today, every Premiership club and many others boast such a facility.

In October 1991 Romanian-born Rodi Woodcock became the first £2 million pools winner.

'Good Old Arsenal' reached number **sixteen** in the charts in 1971 – with words written by Jimmy Hill.

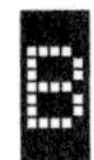

In 1994 Littlewoods became the first ever sponsors of the FA Cup.

In November 1994 regulars from the Yew Tree pub, Greater Manchester, won £2,924,622, but the writing was on the wall for the pools companies as the newly introduced National Lottery savaged their turnover.

Fixed-odds betting continued to grow in popularity, though, and the 1998 World Cup produced the biggest ever betting turnover on a single event, topping even the Grand National, as over £100 million was gambled.

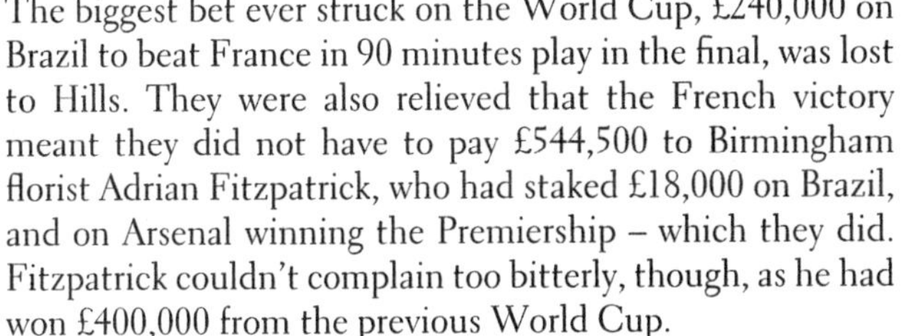

The biggest bet ever struck on the World Cup, £240,000 on Brazil to beat France in 90 minutes play in the final, was lost to Hills. They were also relieved that the French victory meant they did not have to pay £544,500 to Birmingham florist Adrian Fitzpatrick, who had staked £18,000 on Brazil, and on Arsenal winning the Premiership – which they did. Fitzpatrick couldn't complain too bitterly, though, as he had won £400,000 from the previous World Cup.

But if France's World Cup victory was the single best football result of all time for bookmakers, as many claimed, Manchester United's defeat of Bayern Munich in the 1999 European Cup final to complete the Treble was just about the worst, costing the industry some £10 million.

The Canadian Ontario Lottery Corporation allowed gamblers to help themselves to winnings of £365,000 after they continued to take bets on four 1995 English matches which they believed to have evening kick-off times. But the

In April 1998, Real Madrid reached the European Cup final for the first time in **seventeen** years.

matches had taken place during the afternoon and the results were already known to punters with access to the necessary information. As bets were still being accepted, punters were able to stake their wagers already knowing the outcome of the games. Incredibly, the Corporation paid the punters out, with spokesman Don Pister commenting ruefully: 'We have to assume everyone was playing in good faith. The mistake was ours.'

When referee Marcello Cardona abandoned a 1996 Italian second division game in the 89th minute with the scores level, he wasn't aware that by doing so he had prevented a punter from winning £4.8 million on the pools had the game ended in a draw.

Bookie Fred Done is such a keen Manchester United fan that when they beat Chelsea at the end of April 1998 he decided that the race for the Premiership was over – and paid out £50,000 to punters who had backed United to win the title. A few weeks later he was paying out again – to punters who had backed Arsenal, who overhauled United and won the championship.

Paul Gascoigne paid £1,000 to his best friend Jimmy 'Five Bellies' Gardner in August 1998 – after he lost two £500 bets to him. Gazza bet his portly pal £500 a time that he could not take the heat of a cigarette lighter held to his nose for ten seconds. Twice, Five Bellies withstood the flames, which burnt a large mark on his proboscis.

Leeds manager David O'Leary was rapped by the FA in April 1999 after claiming to have placed a £100 bet on Manchester United to win the Premiership.

Against Morocco in 1998, Michael Owen became the youngest player ever to be knocked unconscious while playing for England, at the age of **eighteen**.

A punter from Tadley in Hampshire, who staked £130 on three accumulative bets predicting the winners of all eight English and Scottish Divisions prior to the start of the 1998–99 season, collected £589,308 from Corals.

Bookie Victor Chandler laid claim to taking the biggest recorded gamble on a football match when he told the *Observer* in May 1999 that he once laid a single wager of £1 million on Valencia to beat Barcelona in a Spanish League game. 'The client was on the chase. He got out of trouble,' said Chandler, suggesting that the bet was successful.

I wondered whether Alex Wallace of Glasgow might be psychic after he won a £5 bet at odds of 500/1 that Manchester United would beat Bayern Munich 2–1 in the European Cup final and that Alex Ferguson would subsequently be knighted within a year. He won £2,500.

Fourteen-year-old Jane Wall from North Shields dreamed that her favourite team Newcastle would beat Sheffield Wednesday 8–0 in September 1999. When her dad's workmate Keith Tremble heard of the dream he placed a £2 bet on the result with Ladbrokes, and won £200 – most of which he handed over to happy Jane.

BIAS

Many complain that there are too many pro-Manchester United elements to the game today. But as far back as 1931 the *Daily Express* report of the FA Cup final between WBA and Birmingham ended with the comment: 'Manchester United should have been in the final this year. They could have beaten any team in rain like that.' How disappointing

Finishing bottom of the First Division in season 1911–12, Arsenal's assets were reputed to be **nineteen** pounds.

then, that they weren't there because they had lost in the fourth round – to Grimsby.

BIKE

Pedro Garita cycled from Buenos Aires to Mexico City for the 1986 World Cup final – only to discover when he got there that he could not afford to pay for a ticket. When the 52-year-old returned from the ticket office he found his bike had been stolen.

BLAME

When Rangers lost 3–2 to Hibs in the Scottish Cup quarter-final in 1896, keeper John Bell took it personally, blaming himself to such an extent that he changed without speaking to anyone and walked away from the ground, never to return.

BLIND

Twenty-four-year-old Newbury man Jason Perritt was delighted with his £500 win on the Littlewoods Spot The Ball competition in 1994 – particularly as the banker is blind.

BLOOD

Watford substitute Paul Robinson had to receive treatment despite not having set foot on the pitch as his side scored during April 1998: 'I was so happy that I jumped up and down. Suddenly my nose started to bleed.'

Luton Town fan Sue Miller paid **twenty** pounds to have a tattoo of the club emblem on her left breast.

BOOTS

India had to withdraw from the 1950 World Cup having been refused permission by FIFA to play without boots.

Two brothers broke their legs playing football in the same pair of boots. Jason O'Callaghan, 28, broke his right leg playing for Rassau Rangers in Ebbw Vale, Gwent. He loaned his boots to 34-year-old brother Wayne, who broke his leg playing in them the next weekend in February 1999.

BORDER

Chester City's Deva Stadium, opened in 1992, has a main stand on the east rather than the west side of the ground so that the club offices can be sited on the English side of the border, allowing the club to remain members of the English FA. As soon as anyone steps over the touchline, though, they are in Wales.

BRAINY

Steve Coppell, former Manchester United player and now Crystal Palace boss, has a degree in economics from Liverpool University.

Steve Palmer of Watford boasts a degree in software engineering from Cambridge University.

Iain Dowie of QPR has a degree in mechanical engineering from Hertfordshire University.

Blackburn keeper Tim Flowers, on the subs' bench against Coventry, was sent off without setting foot on the pitch after **twenty-one** minutes for foul and abusive language to a linesman.

Barry Horne of Huddersfield has a degree in chemistry.

Steve Heighway, once of Liverpool, has a degree in economics and politics from Warwick University.

Pat Nevin, late of Chelsea, now of Motherwell, has a degree in commerce.

Tony Galvin, once of Spurs, has a degree in Russian.

Artur Jorge, twice coach of his national side, Portugal, and also of Switzerland for Euro 96, might just be the brainiest chap ever to scale the footballing heights. A Doctor of Philosophy and German Studies, who also speaks French, English, Spanish and Italian, he is also author of a book of poetry – as is, it should be pointed out, John Toshack.

BRAWL

A March 1997 outbreak of mass violence during a World Cup warm-up match between the Jamaican national side and Mexican club Toros Neza, which saw every player plus subs and officials throwing punches and damaging objects, was voted 'The greatest brawl EVER' by *Total Football* magazine.

BULL

Hereford United's May 1999 fundraising idea was bullshit – literally. They sold 1,400 tickets, divided their pitch into squares, then sent Napoleon the bull on to the pitch to

England's 1966 World Cup hat-trick hero, Geoff Hurst, was knighted **twenty-two** years after that triumph.

deposit a mega cow-pat to decide who would win the star prize, an £8,500 Renault Clio car. It went to fan Tim Trible.

BUS

Wolves defender Brian Law was arrested after joyriding a bus through Wolverhampton city centre in July 1995.

Ireland's Mick McCarthy was apparently the 1990 World Cup's dirtiest player, perpetrating **twenty-three** fouls in the course of his five games.

CABBIE

Referee Eleanor Friel, 22, thought that the cabbie who picked her up in Leeds in January 1997 might be interested in her involvement with the game. Instead he told her that she should be at home doing housework instead of reffing matches – and kicked her out of the taxi, a mile away from her home, when she disagreed with him.

CARETAKER

Tony Parkes became permanent manager of Blackburn Rovers in December 1999. He was not without experience in the position – having previously been caretaker boss on no fewer than five occasions. He didn't last long though, and was succeeded by Graeme Souness.

CARROT

Atletico Mineiro striker Edmilson celebrated scoring the opening goal in his side's Brazilian League local derby against

America, known as the Rabbits, by pulling a carrot out of his shorts and ostentatiously eating it in front of their fans.

CARS

Amanda MacNaughton drove on to the pitch during a match and left her car in the goalmouth after discovering that one of the spectators had parked across her drive. The 27-year-old interrupted the November 1998 Beverley, East Riding game between Regency and Long Riston and ref Brian Freeman said, 'I turned around to see this car being driven into the goalmouth. Out got this attractive young woman. Even from 75 yards I could see she was very annoyed.'

Leeds fan Keith Emmerson, 43, from Wakefield, paid £11,000 in September 1999 for the car registration number E11 AND.

Enraged by his players' poor efforts in a 6–1 August 1999 friendly defeat to Gent, Willem II coach Co Adriaanse ordered the team to drive their cars to a village near Tilburg the next day, before confiscating their car keys and making them run the 13 kilometres back to their ground. After lunch he made them run back to pick up their cars.

Mark Statham, keeper of non-league Stalybridge Celtic, missed an early 1999 game after getting his head trapped in a car door.

The experiences of Newcastle fan Gladstone Adams, who drove his car back from a United FA Cup final in 1908, resulted in his invention of the windscreen wiper! Caught in hail whilst returning, Adams improvised a mechanical device

Michael Owen took **twenty-five** strides from first touch to last as he scored his 'goal of the century' against Argentina in the 1998 World Cup.

to clear his windows, which he then worked on and perfected – to the benefit of all future motorists.

Stockport County physio Roger Wylde made striker Ian Moore sell his Porsche to cure his knee injury. Said Wylde of the low-slung £34,000 wheels: 'Getting in and out of the car was putting stress on the injury, straining the inside of the knee and pushing the leg outwards.'

Players at Mansfield Town had to wash cars to raise money to pay for an overnight stay when they visited Torquay for a Third Division game in March 1999.

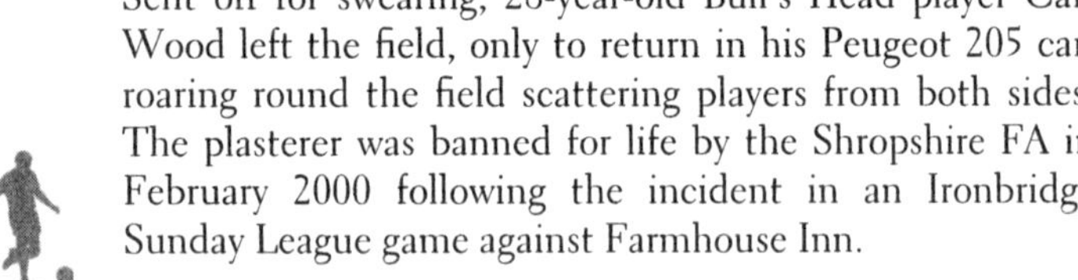

Sent off for swearing, 28-year-old Bull's Head player Carl Wood left the field, only to return in his Peugeot 205 car, roaring round the field scattering players from both sides. The plasterer was banned for life by the Shropshire FA in February 2000 following the incident in an Ironbridge Sunday League game against Farmhouse Inn.

CELEBRITIES

Eat your heart out, David Beckham – in 1958 England skipper Billy Wright, of Wolves, married Joy, one of the hugely popular Beverley Sisters, chart-toppers of the day.

A poll amongst Welsh fans to discover who was their choice to succeed Bobby Gould as manager in 1999 saw Ian Rush pick up seven per cent of the votes – just behind Shirley Bassey.

Madonna and Sean Penn, starring in the 1986 film *Shanghai*

Surprise, featured in a scene supposedly set in Joe Go's contraband warehouse – which was actually filmed in the Stevenage Road stand at Fulham's Craven Cottage ground.

Pop star Morrissey's bedroom was dominated by a massive, framed photograph of English football icon Bobby Moore.

Geoffrey Boycott was once a director of Melchester Rovers – Roy (of the Rovers) Race's club.

BBC Radio's cult commentator Stuart Hall, late of *It's A Knockout* fame, played for Crystal Palace reserves in 1953.

Music hall entertainer George Robey was on Chelsea's books, making one reserve appearance against Hastings.

Alan Simpson, half of the renowned comic writing duo Galton & Simpson who created the Steptoes, was due to sign for Chelsea as a keeper in 1947, only to contract tuberculosis before he could put pen to paper.

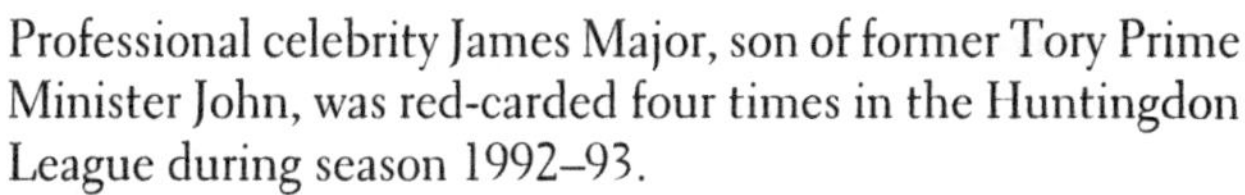

Professional celebrity James Major, son of former Tory Prime Minister John, was red-carded four times in the Huntingdon League during season 1992–93.

Michael Jackson turned up to watch Fulham play in the Second Division during the 1998–99 season. In 1991 he refused to permit Wycombe Wanderers to use a parody of the old Dion hit 'The Wanderer' at their games, as he owned the rights to the music.

Admitted to the Football League in 1921, Southport did not have a single player sent off in one thousand and **twenty-seven** games, until 18 October 1952 when Walter Taylor was dismissed.

Readers of *Penthouse* magazine were surprised to read a 1993 interview with great German player Franz Beckenbauer in which he revealed he would like to come back as a woman, while readers of *Playboy* wondered at claims by Pele, who said: 'Boys and girls confined to wheelchairs start walking again after I visit them in hospitals.'

Rock group Massive Attack have claimed to support both Bristol City and Bristol Rovers.

Celebrating victory over Orient in November 1991, the Torquay team were joined in the bath by striker Justin Fashanu's 'girlfriend', actress Julie 'Bet Lynch' Goodyear.

CELEBRITY DIRECTORS

Aldershot . . . Arthur English (1981–90)
Birmingham City . . . Jasper Carrott (1979–82)
Brighton & Hove Albion . . . Norman Wisdom (1970–78)
Charlton Athletic . . . Michael Grade (Current)
Chelsea . . . Lord Richard Attenborough (1969–82)
Leyton Orient . . . Steve Davis (Current)
Portsmouth . . . Fred Dinenage (Current)
Rochdale . . . Tommy Cannon (1986–87)
Swindon Town . . . Willie Carson (Current)
Watford . . . Sir Elton John (1973–90; current)

CELEBRITY FANS

Arsenal . . . Reggie Kray, Johnny Rotten, Ray Davies, Stanley Kubrick, Frankie Dettori
Aston Villa . . . Floella Benjamin
Blackpool . . . The Nolans

5–1 down, with ten men, with **twenty-eight** minutes left, Charlton beat Huddersfield 7–6 in their December 1957 game, leaving their opponents the only side to lose a League game having scored six goals.

Burnley . . . Sir Edward Heath
Charlton Athletic . . . Jim Davidson, Mick Jagger
Chelsea . . . Racquel Welch
Crystal Palace . . . Jo Brand, Roy Hudd
Leeds United . . . Stefan Edberg
Leicester City . . . Engelbert Humperdinck
Liverpool . . . Austin Powers, alias Mike Myers
Manchester United . . . Mick Hucknall
Northampton Town . . . Des O'Connor
Norwich City . . . Stephen Fry
Port Vale . . . Robbie Williams
Queen's Park Rangers . . . Bill Wyman
Swansea City . . . Catherine Zeta Jones
Tottenham Hotspur . . . Chris Eubank
Tranmere Rovers . . . Glenda Jackson

CHAIR

A five-legged chair which stands in the Arsenal boardroom is said to have been purchased specially for a gout-affected director who would rise rapidly from his normal seat, invariably knocking it backwards.

CHANTS

'Sing when you're whaling, you only sing when you're whaling.' Scotland supporters to Norwegian counterparts at World Cup '98.

Not noted for his svelte, greyhound-like appearance, ex-striker Mick Quinn is generally believed to be the inspiration for the now-familiar refrain, 'He's fat, he's round, He scores on every ground . . .', first instigated by Coventry supporters.

Inverness Thistle's second-round Scottish Cup tie against Falkirk was postponed **twenty-nine** times before being played on 22 February 1979.

Chelsea fans paid attention when their hero, French World Cup star Frank Leboeuf, requested them not to swear whilst chanting his name, and revised their tribute to: 'He's here, he's there, We're not allowed to swear, Frank Leboeuf . . .'

Arsenal fans rapidly came up with an appropriate chant for their French World Cup star Emmanuel Petit: 'He's blond, he's quick, His name's a porno flick, Emmanuel . . .'

They followed this up with their tribute to lanky genius Nwankwo Kanu, who once had surgery to repair a faulty cardiac valve: 'He's big, he's black, He's had a heart attack, he's Kanu, he's Kanu . . .'

University of Munster researcher Bernd Strauss published a 1999 study claiming to show that chanting, singing and abuse by crowds had no influence on the outcome of football matches. 'If nothing else, it makes the spectators feel better,' declared Herr Strauss, who visited precisely four matches to draw his conclusions.

Some terrace chants which are derived from chart hits . . .
Go West (Pet Shop Boys) . . . '1–0 to the Arsenal . . .'
Sailing (Rod Stewart) . . . 'No one likes us, we don't care . . .'
Son of my Father (Chicory Tip) . . . 'Oh, Teddy, Teddy . . .'
Hooray, It's a Holi-Holiday (Boney M) . . . 'He gets the ball, he scores a goal . . .'
Mary's Boy Child (Boney M) . . . 'Hark now, hear the —— sing . . .'
Hello Hello (I'm Back Again) (Gary Glitter) . . . '—— are back, —— are back . . .'
Oops Upside Your Head (Gap Band) . . . 'Ooh, aah, Cantona . . .'

A referee's whistle used in the nineteen-**thirty** FA Cup final was sold for £1,000 at Sotheby's in July 1998.

Daydream Believer (Monkees) . . . 'Cheer up Peter Reid . . .'
Guantanamera (Sandpipers) . . . 'One ——, there's only one —— . . .'
Que Sera Sera (Doris Day) . . . 'We're going to Wemberley . . .'

CHIMP

Dorchester Town of the Dr Martens League elected a new honorary director in February 1999 – a chimpanzee called Trudy which had been rescued from a circus where it was being ill-treated.

CLAPPING

When Afghanistan's national football team was permitted to reform in May 1998 after a three-year absence, the country's ruling Taliban party declared in the *Afghan Online Press* that 'onlookers will not be permitted to clap, but will be ordered to encourage both sides equally with cheers of "Allahu Akbar". Players will also need to be modestly dressed with long trousers and sleeves.'

A Real Madrid fan had to go to court to have a nine-month ban from the ground and a £3 fine lifted in 1962. His crime? Applauding when the opposition scored, which had produced a letter from the club: 'You must not encourage our opponents.'

COLOURS

Devastated after Rangers lost the 1997–98 Scottish League title to great rivals Celtic, David Pickett flew off to America.

The 1967 match between Cardiff and Millwall was abandoned after **thirty-one** minutes, when a Millwall fan punched Cardiff boss Jimmy Scoular on the jaw.

On returning to his bungalow in Gourock, Renfrewshire, he discovered that friends had painted it in green and white hoops.

John Roddy was baffled when he went to watch Everton play Sheffield Wednesday in April 1998 – because he couldn't see the ball. Red-green colourblind fan John was unable to follow the action because an experimental yellow ball was being used.

Juventus adopted their famous black and white stripes in 1903 after one of their committee members visited England and saw Notts County turn out in those colours.

Before adopting their famous red strip in 1898, Liverpool spent five years in blue and white quartered shirts.

After three years of trying, a Bradford City fan succeeded in 1999 in breeding a primula in the club's amber and claret colours.

The very first incarnation of what would emerge as Manchester City played in 1884 at Pink Bank Lane in black jerseys with a white cross.

COMMENTATORS

'Football commentators are knowingly and gratuitously illiterate.' Damning criticism by Poet Laureate Andrew Motion, reported by the *Daily Telegraph* on 23 June 1999.

Bobby Charlton was booked for the first time in international football – **thirty-two** years after the match. It was only discovered in 1998 that Charlton had been cautioned during England's 1966 World Cup game against Argentina.

CORACLE

Fred Davies, who died in November 1994 aged 83, was one of the great unsung heroes of British football – having for 45 years used his coracle to rescue footballs kicked out of Shrewsbury's ground into the River Severn. He earned between 25p and 50p per ball, and his record haul in a single season was 130. He retired in 1986.

CORNER

In his book *The Story of Football*, first published in 1952, William Lowndes reports the story of a player who scored without ever setting foot on the pitch. 'In 1937 two amateur sides played a minor cup-tie. The outside left of one team was late in arriving, and when he stripped, the game had started. As he stood on the touchline awaiting the referee's permission to join the game his team attacked and forced a corner. The referee acknowledged his arrival and waved to him to take the corner kick. He did so, and scored direct!'

COWARD

'My instinctive reaction was to walk away,' England star Matt Le Tissier told a judge during a 1999 trial involving an attack on him in a Southampton nightclub.

'Is that your training?' asked the judge.

'No,' replied Le Tiss. 'It's just being a coward.'

CRIME

Thieves who raided the changing rooms while a game was going on at Brampton FC's ground near Huntingdon in November 1999, realised they had made a big mistake when

Third Division Mansfield had to wait for eight hundred and **thirty-three** minutes of football on their own pitch before scoring on 18 December against Plymouth in 1972–73.

they were pounced on by 23 policemen – who had been playing in the game between Cambridgeshire Police and the Met's NW Division.

CRISPS

Following Manchester United's completion of the Treble, crisp makers Walkers claimed they received 5,000 calls begging them to introduce Smoky Beckham crisps.

Everton refused to stock Walkers' 'Cheese 'n' Owen' crisps during the 1998–99 season because they were named after Liverpool striker Michael Owen.

CUPS

Morpeth Harriers received Cup winners' medals without even playing in the final of the 1886 Northumberland Cup. Shankhouse beat Newcastle West End in the final, having come through the semi-final against Morpeth in extraordinary circumstances. The two sides met five times in a replayed semi. In the fourth match a spectator blew a whistle which caused Morpeth to stop playing and allowed Shankhouse to score for a 3–2 lead, but the FA overruled the goal and ordered a fifth meeting.

'This game went on so long,' said a report of the time, 'that two referees were used – the first left to catch a train – and, four hours after the kick-off, darkness stopped play with the sides still level. The teams had now played for 10½ hours and it was agreed to toss up to see which club should go forward' – on condition that if it was successful in the final, the Cup would be held jointly. Shankhouse won the toss, the final – and Morpeth won their medals.

Egypt's goalkeeper in the nineteen **thirty-four** World Cup? Mustafa Kamel Mansour.

Passed off for two years as the real thing after England won the World Cup in 1966, a replica Jules Rimet Trophy was sold for £254,500 at Sotheby's in July 1997.

The second leg of the final of the inaugural Industrial Inter-City Fairs Cup, which would become the UEFA Cup, was played on 1 May 1958 – almost three years after the first game in the tournament on 4 June 1955 when London beat Basle. Barcelona won the first competition.

Sir Francis Marindin, President of the FA, refereed the 1887 FA Cup semi-final between WBA and Preston, the latter featuring a number of Scots in their line-up. After the game, Marindin entered the victorious WBA dressing room and asked, 'Are you all Englishmen?' Being answered in the affirmative, he announced: 'Then I have very much pleasure in presenting you with the ball and I hope you win the Cup.'

Asked about a plan to stage the World Cup every two years, Rangers goalkeeper Lionel Charbonnier commented: 'It is like a woman – the longer you wait for one, the more you appreciate it. Every four years is fine.'

Scientists announced in February 1999 that they had constructed a replica World Cup consisting of just a single molecule, measuring three nanometres – less than a ten-millionth the size of the real, 14-inch-high cup. They did not, apparently, announce why.

'There is no club which the Celts would rather see win the Cup than Rangers.' Celtic president John Glass in, er . . . 1893.

Fulham's record attendance of forty nine thousand, three hundred and **thirty-five** was set v Millwall in Division Two on 8 October 1938.

'I told the players that the cup would be six feet away from them at the end of the game, and that if they lost they wouldn't even touch it.' Alex Ferguson's half-time team talk to Manchester United, who were a goal down to Bayern Munich in 1999's European Cup final, but went on to win it.

Aston Villa and Rotherham reached the final of the 1960–61 League Cup – but the two-legged decider didn't take place until the 1961–62 season, with Villa winning 3–2 on aggregate.

CURRY

Ten Scotland fans, in Bordeaux to follow their side during the 1998 World Cup, spent £600 on a takeaway order of curry and lager from the Eye of the Tiger restaurant in Bournemouth, plus £800 on a charter flight to deliver it. 'We support Scotland now,' said restaurant boss Mustafa Aolad.

CURSED

Researching for a 1996 book on local legends, journalist Michael Goss discovered that a number of football grounds are claimed to have been cursed.

Goss claims that Leeds United manager Don Revie had a Blackpool fortune teller in to exorcise Elland Road in 1972, and that Derby did likewise in 1946. Preston hired a gypsy – Paula Paradema – to perform ritual magic just before the 1994–95 season, who 'claimed to have placed an archangel in each corner of Deepdale'.

At non-league Dorchester Town the story is that a 'homemade wizard', otherwise a computer businessman, cursed the ground whilst intending to affect 'environmental despoilation' of land nearby, but that the football ground

was 'accidentally caught in the psychic fall-out'.

At Gillingham a hex was allegedly placed on the club – beaten in extraordinary circumstances in the 1999 Second Division play-off final – by 'a person who blamed a recent bereavement on the club'.

At Birmingham, then manager Barry Fry is famously said to have urinated in each corner of the St Andew's ground in an effort to ward off evil spirits, while it is also said that former boss Ron Saunders had the soles of his players' boots painted red and had a priest exorcise the ground – all a waste of time according to Goss, who uncovered evidence that the curse was actually lifted when a fan transferred it during building work to bitter rivals Aston Villa!

Goss concluded his researches convinced that these were generally self-perpetuating myths: 'Fabricated folklore, ersatz traditions, can become the genuine article if the folk – in this case the fans – decide to accept them as genuine.'

A witch-doctor clad in just a loincloth and balancing a pot on his head urinated on the pitch prior to Ivory Coast's 1993 World Cup qualifier against Nigeria. It did the trick – they won 2–1.

Desperate to improve their fading fortunes, Brazilian second division side Nautico reportedly sacrificed a bull as part of a seven-day ritual overseen by Umbanda priest Father Edu in February 1999.

A dead black chicken with its throat cut was recently discovered in the directors' box at Colombian club Deportes Pereira, while bags of soil from a nearby cemetery were also brought into the ground to ward off poor performances. The club lost 13 of their next 14 matches.

Peruvian team Melgar were cursed by a former player in 1979, and began to slip down the table – until they had their kit washed in a potion designed to ward off evil spirits. It seemed to do the trick as they avoided relegation in a play-off.

Labouring under the handicap of a gypsy's curse – apparently provoked by the moving on of gypsies from the land on which their ground was developed – Derby County lost the 1898 FA Cup final to Nottingham Forest 3–1. The gypsies obviously weren't satisfied by this – as Derby were again beaten in the 1899 final, then humiliated by Bury 6–0 in the 1903 final.

After a run of just three wins from 12 home games in 1993, Derby County called in clairvoyant Adeline Lee to remove the reported gypsy curse on the ground. They won eight of their next 11 home matches.

The Valley Party contested the 1990 local government elections in Greenwich to support Charlton's efforts to return to their old ground – and polled fourteen thousand, eight hundred and **thirty-eight** votes.

DEBUT

Half-back Alf Day, who signed for Spurs in 1931, made his international debut for Wales before turning out for his debut first-team League game.

Albert Tennant signed on for Chelsea in November 1934, and made his League debut in May 1947.

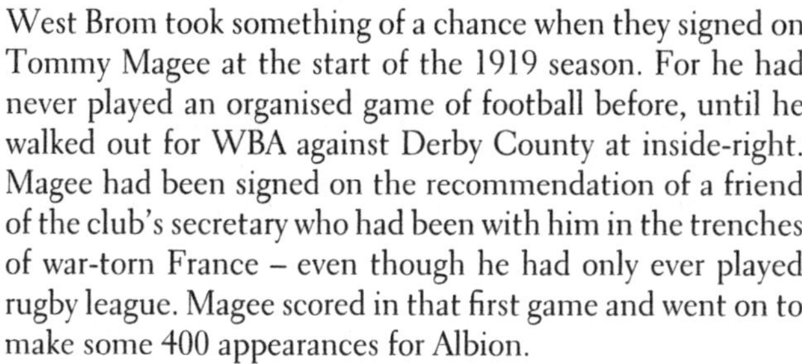

West Brom took something of a chance when they signed on Tommy Magee at the start of the 1919 season. For he had never played an organised game of football before, until he walked out for WBA against Derby County at inside-right. Magee had been signed on the recommendation of a friend of the club's secretary who had been with him in the trenches of war-torn France – even though he had only ever played rugby league. Magee scored in that first game and went on to make some 400 appearances for Albion.

When Stan Mortensen made his international debut he did

Dixie Dean scored a record 60 goals in **thirty-nine** games for Everton during the 1927–28 League season.

so against his own country. Stan was a reserve for England who were playing Wales at Wembley on 25 September 1943. At half-time, injured Welsh left-half Powell was unable to continue, so Stan took his place.

DISGUISE

When *Aberdeen Evening Express* football writer Charlie Allan was banned from covering the Dons' match against Dundee United by United boss Tommy McLean after writing a critical article, his paper came up with a cunning plan to get round the situation. They printed free cut-out-and-keep masks of the reporter, which were worn by hundreds of fans entering the ground – including Allan himself.

DOGS

As West Ham were playing Liverpool in April 1972 a dog invaded the pitch, stopping the game as he cocked his leg against Liverpool keeper Ray Clemence's post before being sent packing.

Nottingham Forest skipper Steve Chettle was described as 'brave but stupid' by police in November 1999 after diving into the River Trent at a point known for dangerous under-currents whilst wearing full training kit, to rescue a drowning dog. Afterwards Chettle commented: 'I don't even like dogs.'

In the 1985 Staffordshire Sunday Cup the referee awarded a goal for Knave of Clubs against Newcastle Town after the ball was bundled over the line by a dog who ran on to the pitch.

Barnsley defender Darren Barnard was out injured for a month during the 1998–99 season after aggravating a knee problem. He slipped on a floor made wet when his dog weed on it.

South Korea's government postponed a decision on the legalisation of dog meat until after it hosted the 2002 World Cup 'to spare any embarrassment during the tournament'.

Brentford keeper Chic Brodie's career was ended in 1970 when he suffered knee damage following a collision during a match against Colchester – with a dog.

Feyenoord fan Jan van Kook, 33, bought a season ticket for his pet dog, Bo, for the Dutch side's 1998–99 campaign.

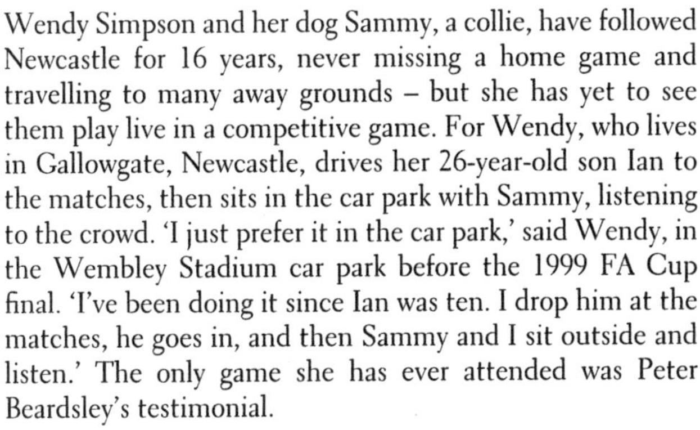

Wendy Simpson and her dog Sammy, a collie, have followed Newcastle for 16 years, never missing a home game and travelling to many away grounds – but she has yet to see them play live in a competitive game. For Wendy, who lives in Gallowgate, Newcastle, drives her 26-year-old son Ian to the matches, then sits in the car park with Sammy, listening to the crowd. 'I just prefer it in the car park,' said Wendy, in the Wembley Stadium car park before the 1999 FA Cup final. 'I've been doing it since Ian was ten. I drop him at the matches, he goes in, and then Sammy and I sit outside and listen.' The only game she has ever attended was Peter Beardsley's testimonial.

DOUBLE BOOKING

Awarded a benefit match in 1910 after playing 199 games in

Record scorer of League goals in the Third Division North was Mansfield's Ted Harston who, in 1936–37, hit 55 in **forty-one** games.

seven seasons for Birmingham, right-back Frank Stokes was unable to appear in the game – as he was selected for a reserve match on the same afternoon.

DRIVING

Cabbie Will Redford, 52, picked up three West Ham fans from Aldershot – and took them to see the Hammers play Metz in France in August 1999, for a round trip fare of £390. Phil Carter, Colin Stein and Rob Collins gladly shelled out, leaving at 10 a.m. and returning by 4 a.m. the next morning – with an InterToto aggregate victory to cheer.

Spotting a chauffeur-driven Mercedes Benz in Sao Paulo in October 1999, a gunman held it up when it stopped at traffic lights, demanding jewellery and cash. However, when he recognised Pelé sitting in the back with his wife Assyna, the thief put his gun down, apologised and left.

Thanks to his fear of flying, Arsenal striker Dennis Bergkamp endured a two-day car journey of 1,100 miles in order to play for his side in the Champions' League against Fiorentina in September 1999.

Liverpool's Jan Molby was given a three-month sentence in February 1988 for driving at 100 mph in a 30 mph area, going through two sets of red lights and driving on the wrong side of the road.

DRUGS

Illegal substances are the scourge of many sports these days,

Of **forty-two** matches played by Norwich in the 1978–79 First Division season, they drew a record 23.

but they are nothing new – although maybe a little more effective than those administered to Arsenal players prior to a 1924–25 FA Cup first round game against West Ham. An hour before kick-off, the players took 'pep-pills' designed to supply 'extra punch and stamina'. But the game was subsequently abandoned due to fog: 'The pills left a bitter taste, a raging thirst and pent-up energy for which there was no outlet.' The match was rescheduled for two days later, and exactly the same thing happened. The third attempt was a little more successful. The game ended goalless, but 'the hard match accentuated the thirst and bitter taste so much that players had a most uncomfortable night', refusing to take the pills again.

A survey carried out by the *Independent* newspaper in December 1998 purported to show that 22 per cent of the 'top level' footballers who responded had tried cannabis, 9 per cent had tried ecstasy and 7 per cent cocaine.

Robbie Fowler was fined two weeks' wages by Liverpool and charged with misconduct by the FA in April 1999 after controversially acting out a cocaine-sniffing-style goal celebration against Everton.

Forty-three of the scheduled 46 Football League fixtures were postponed because of bad weather on 1 January 1979.

EARLY DAYS

Tottenham Hotspur were formed in 1882 when they played at Tottenham Marsh and held their committee meetings under a lamp-post in Northumberland Park.

Reports of an early local derby between Middlesbrough and Old Tyne of Newcastle recorded: 'The Middlesbrough ranks were badly depleted. Only seven players were left, the other four having been carried off.'

Amateur player Hill Drury, from Darlington, who played for Middlesbrough at the end of the 19th century, always insisted upon paying the admission fee to get into the grounds where he was playing.

An FA report in 1899 by Sir Charles Clegg, Mr C. Crump and Mr C.W. Alcock concluded that 'The practice of buying and selling players is unsportsmanlike and most objectionable.'

Eric Nixon played **forty-four** games in season 1986–87 – in the process becoming the first player to play in all four divisions of the Football League in the same season.

When they were founded in 1883, Coventry City were the works team of bicycle, and later car, manufacturers, Singer.

The Scottish Film and Television Archive in Edinburgh were proud of their vintage film from 1908 showing the earliest recorded example of Scottish football – a game between Leith Athletic of Edinburgh, and unidentified opponents. Until November 1999, that is, when Napier University football historian Tom Poole examined the film in great detail and revealed it to be of the 1912 English FA Cup final at Crystal Palace between Barnsley and WBA.

EGG

During a 1998 Second Division play-off game at Fulham, Grimsby keeper Aidan Davison was felled by a hard-boiled egg.

EMBROIDERY

Even in those days it must have been a little unusual that Billy Wright, the first man to win 100 caps for England, would confess in the fifties that his hobbies were rug-making and embroidery and that in music 'his taste is for opera'.

EXCUSES

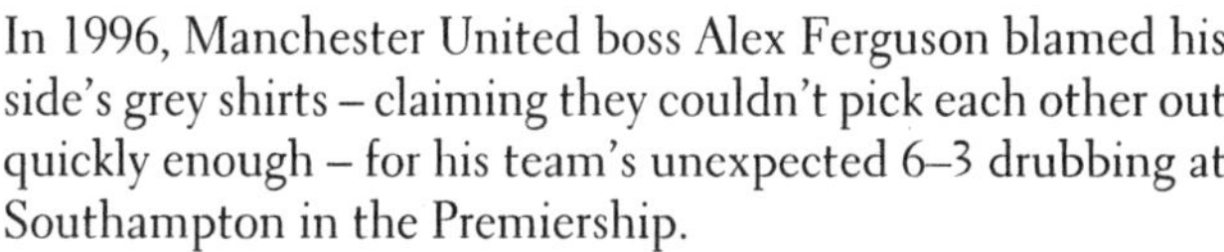

In 1996, Manchester United boss Alex Ferguson blamed his side's grey shirts – claiming they couldn't pick each other out quickly enough – for his team's unexpected 6–3 drubbing at Southampton in the Premiership.

On 17 January 1987, 37 of the **forty-five** scheduled Football League games were postponed.

And when United's Italian keeper Massimo Taibi let a long shot from Southampton's Matt Le Tissier squirm through his hands and legs and over the line in September 1999, he blamed the length of his studs.

Chelsea delayed a press conference during the 1998–99 season, citing the remarkable excuse: 'Mr Vialli is shaving his head.'

Beaten in the 1887 FA Cup final by Aston Villa, a West Bromwich Albion official came up with a splendid excuse. A Mr Smith, secretary of the Throstles, explained that prior to the game Albion had gone away to Ascot to prepare: 'We have discovered since the match that the air at Ascot was not bracing enough. It was what might be termed "softening". It tended to reduce the stamina of the men.'

Reading boss Alan Pardew blamed the yellow ball – used to enhance TV pictures – for his side's November 1999 home defeat by Oxford. 'Those balls are very springy, and that didn't help us,' he moaned.

Through on goal during a match against St Albans in 1886, Luton Town's star striker Frank Whitby missed 'abysmally'. His excuse? The smoke from the engine of a passing train blinded him.

Chesterfield set a Football League record by scoring in **forty-six** consecutive League games from 25 December 1929 to 26 December 1930.

FAIRGROUND

Legendary goalkeeper Willie 'Fatty' Foulke, the 20-stone-plus Sheffield United and Chelsea player, spent the years prior to his death in 1916 touring with a fairground, charging all comers to take him on in penalty prize competitions. He was so huge that an opponent once suggested that the outline of an average-sized keeper should be etched on to him and that if the ball hit outside that line a goal should be awarded.

FAMILY

Leeds' team during the 1996–97 season included Ian Harte and his uncle, Gary Kelly.

Leicester's Arni and Preston's Bjarki Gunnlaugsson became probably the first ever Icelandic twins to play simultaneously in the English League, during the 1999–2000 season.

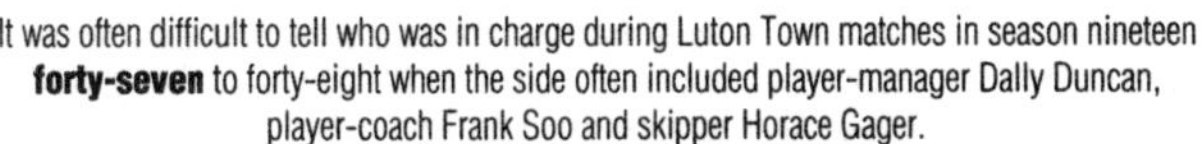

Bolton striker Eidur Gudjohnsen has a claim to an historic achievement – appearing in the same international side as his father. When Eidur came on as a sub for Iceland, it was to replace dad Arnar. Injury prevented the pair of them appearing from the start in an international together.

FANS

Reg Weston, named as Stockport County's top fan in 1991, left his pregnant wife to run off with the promotions girl who organised the competition.

Reading fan David Downs bottled the soapy water left after the kit used in the club's 1988 Simod Cup victory at Wembley was washed. In 1998, after Reading finished playing at Elm Park prior to moving to the Madejski Stadium, he pitched a tent in the centre circle and stayed there overnight.

German Ebby Kleinrensing was named Nottingham Forest fan of the season, after spending £15,000 flying from Düsseldorf to watch every game of their 1998–99 campaign.

Manchester United are one of the best supported teams in the world – but also one of the most disliked, the success of an organisation formed in 1992 by Irish broadcaster Des Cahill, presenter of the RTE *Breakfast Show*, confirms. The ABU – Anybody But United – club boasts a T-shirt featuring lists of sides such as York and Galatasaray which have inflicted embarrassing defeats on United, and Cahill says that the more successful United become, the more members he acquires. He, bizarrely, is a West Ham supporter.

The theme tune of the ABU, played on the show every morning following a United defeat, is 'Zip A Dee Doo-Dah'.

Scottish international Tommy Walker played **forty-eight** League games in 1946–47 – 9 with Hearts, 39 in Division One for Chelsea, a record equalled in 1974–75 by Dick Habbin with 27 for Reading, 21 for Rotherham.

Presumably, ABU members all own copies of Colin Schindler's big-selling 1998 book, *Manchester United Ruined My Life*.

FASHION

Fans of Brazilian side Fluminense Rio de Janeiro wear white face powder as a symbol of their support for the club nicknamed Po de Arroz – face powder – after a turn of the (19th) century fashion.

FEMALES

Carolina Morace, the first female coach of a men's professional team in Italy, quit Serie C side Viterbese after just two matches – having won the first, but lost the second 5–2 at Crotone. She said she resigned after club owner Luciano Gaucci wanted to fire her assistant coach, Betty Bavagnoli, in September 1999. 'It shows a lack of faith in me,' said Signora Morace, who played 150 games for the Italian women's side. It was a shame she packed it in – after all, the club had painted its stand pink and decorated it with flowers before their opening match of the season, in which the attendance – averaging 100 the season before – was 367.

Golfer Laura Davies has her own five-a-side soccer pitch at home. She is so keen on football that she once carried a pocket-size TV around with her during the final round of a tournament in Spain to watch England play, and still won the event.

A nutritionist who had advised Alan Shearer on his diet for two years admitted that her qualifications were completely

bogus during a September 1999 court case. Twenty-eight-year-old Sue Ready, who joined Newcastle United in 1996, had forged her certificates. She was put on probation for two years and told to pay £300 in compensation.

A Madrid bar owner, Margarita Peces, formed the Association of Women Abandoned for Football in September 1996 as a protest against saturation coverage of the game on TV. Members withdrew certain marital privileges, including ironing, cooking and shopping.

The *Daily Record* revealed that a June 1996 women's match in Sora, Italy, ended in uproar when it was discovered that the keeper of one side was a man wearing a wig.

Celebrating the 28th anniversary of their Page Three Girl feature in November 1998, the *Sun* revealed that of the 1,941 girls pictured thus far, 388 of them had dated footballers.

Camberwell Old Fallopians Women's Football Club must be contenders for the most controversially named club in the game. In 1996 the side, playing at South Bank University Sports Ground in London, adopted the chant 'Up the Tubes' which, according to match secretary Jennifer Cole, 'we tried unsuccessfully to market to Tampax in an attempt to get sponsorship'.

Third Lanark FC, which went into liquidation in 1967, was revived in August 1999 as a women's team in the SWFA third division.

During the year 1965, Sir Stanley Matthews became the only player aged **fifty** ever to compete in the First Division, when turning out for Stoke.

The England men's coach is certainly a confirmed fan of the ladies' game, as Kevin Keegan, who has coached Fulham Ladies FC, told the *Guardian*. 'There is no difference. In fact, some of the girls can do things men would find very difficult to do. When I coached at the Centre of Excellence, one girl in particular had a trick I'd never seen any professional do before.'

FENG SHUI

After Manchester City found themselves in the Second Division at the end of the 1998–99 season, feng shui expert Lindsay Reade claimed that their decline was due to City bosses' lack of attention to the laws of the ancient Chinese science, which focuses on the layout of homes and offices to create a healthy environment. 'The position of the whole ground is bad,' said Reade. 'The street heading straight towards the main entrance is classic poor feng shui.' She accused the stand of emanating 'malign energy . . . the worst thing about it is not the height but the sharp angle of the metal framework directed towards the pitch. It resembles a blade attacking the pitch.'

So, how to explain their recent revival? – although they won the 2nd Division play-off final at Wembley, not at home.

FINE

Palermo player Graziano Ladoni was fined almost £700 in February 1971 – allegedly for failing to say goodbye to his manager.

Southend defender Leo Roget was fined a week's wages in December 1999 – for trashing opponents Barnet's ghetto-blaster when the visitors turned it up after winning 3–1 at Roots Hall in a Third Division game.

Neil McBain made his debut for Third Division North side New Brighton in goal on 15 March 1947 – at the age of **fifty-one** years and four months, making him both the oldest debutant and the oldest player to appear in a Football League match.

FIRE

When John Hartson joined Wimbledon from West Ham in a £7.5m move during the 1998–99 season, his new team-mates welcomed him by setting fire to his suit in the dressing room. He wasn't wearing it at the time.

FIRSTS

Football's first referee's whistle was used during a match between soldiers of the Shropshire Regiment and Maltese locals from Cospicua St Andrew's when they drew 1–1 on the George Cross Island in 1886.

Steve Watts was the first player to join a club after winning a national newspaper competition. Watts, 22, was amongst 850 wannabee pros who entered the *Sun*'s 'Search for a Striker' competition, with the reward of a professional contract at Orient the star prize. He signed for the club in October 1998 and appeared at Wembley Stadium as the Os narrowly lost out to Scunthorpe in the 1999 Division Three play-off final.

The Football League's first sponsored competition was the Watney's Cup, contested between the two top-scoring clubs in each division. It was first played for in 1971 – and won by Colchester United.

Spain were the first Wembley visitors to play under lights – they came on 73 minutes into a game kicking off one afternoon in November 1955.

Charlie Wallace of Aston Villa was the first man to miss an

Top scorer of League goals in the Fourth Division prior to its 1992 restructuring was Peterborough's Terry Bly with **fifty-two** in 46 1960–61 games.

FA Cup final penalty, but Villa still beat Sunderland 1–0 to lift the trophy.

Paul Scholes opened the scoring for England at Hampden Park in the Euro 2000 play-off first leg against Scotland – and was booked for over-celebration, an international first for his country.

James Oakes was the first player to play for both sides in a single game. He turned out for Port Vale as they took on Charlton on Boxing Day 1932, but as the weather closed in the game was abandoned. By the time it was rearranged Oakes had become a Charlton player.

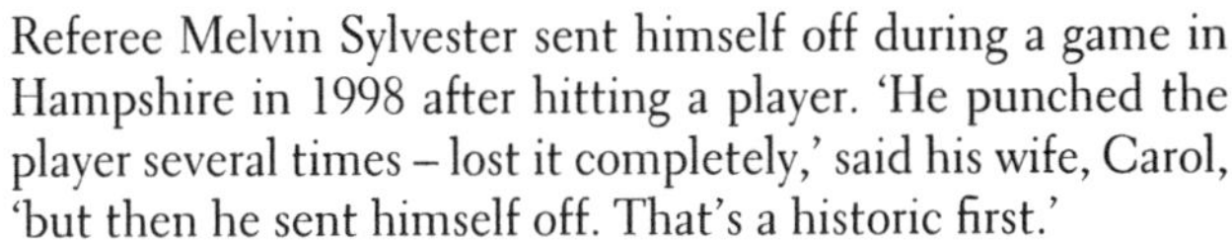

Referee Melvin Sylvester sent himself off during a game in Hampshire in 1998 after hitting a player. 'He punched the player several times – lost it completely,' said his wife, Carol, 'but then he sent himself off. That's a historic first.'

He was banned for six weeks, but commented, 'At least I'm not as bad as the African ref who got so fed up that he shot one of the players.'

The first self-confessed professional footballer is Scot J.J. Lang, who moved from his native country where he played for Clydesdale and Glasgow Eastern, to play for Sheffield Wednesday in 1876.

Hitachi, the Japanese electronics company, were the first commercial concern to sign a shirt sponsorship deal with an English League club – however, Liverpool were not permitted to wear the logo in televised matches in 1979 when the deal was done.

Diego Maradona was fouled **fifty-three** times during the 1990 World Cup finals, during which he played seven games.

Keeper Steve Milton had an unhappy Third Division North debut for Halifax in 1934, conceding 13 goals against Stockport.

In 1988 Dave Beasant of Wimbledon became both the first keeper to captain his team to victory in an FA Cup final and the first keeper to save a penalty in a Wembley FA Cup final.

The first 'golden goal' was scored by Brazil in the 13th minute of additional extra time, after the usual 90 minutes plus 30 minutes extra time failed to produce a result in the 1919 Copa America final in which they beat Uruguay.

The first club to play in the Premiership, all four divisions of the Football League, and both sections (North and South) of Division Three, are Coventry. Grimsby will match them if they reach the Premiership.

FIXTURE CONGESTION

Leyton FC, currently of the Ryman League Division One, reached the Amateur Cup final on 26 April 1952 – which led to something of a fixture pile-up, as they then had to complete their Athenian League programme by playing Hendon on the 28th, Sutton on the 29th, Wealdstone on the 30th, Finchley on 1 May, Enfield on 2 May and Southall on 3 May.

WBA were busy in April 1912, playing seven games in ten days – two of them FA Cup finals. After drawing 0–0 with Barnsley in the Cup final on 20 April they lost 3–0 at Everton in Division One on 22 April. Two days later their replay

The Pools Panel's most hectic afternoon's work came on 27 January 1996 when they had to adjudicate on **fifty-four** matches.

against Barnsley went to extra time, in which they conceded the only goal of the game. On the 25th they lost 4–1 at Blackburn and 24 hours later they drew 0–0 at home to Bradford City, the next day going down 5–1 at home to Sheffield Wednesday before, on the 29th, sharing a goalless draw at home with Oldham.

Redditch United of the Dr Martens League faced a busy end to the 1997–98 season. On Saturday 25 April they lost 2–1 at Wisbech. On the 26th they played at Brackley, on the 27th against Corby and on the 28th they met Halesowen in the Birmingham Senior Cup final. On Wednesday 29 April they had to play against Ilkeston and on the 30th against Stourbridge, on Friday 1 May against Warwick and on Saturday 2 May against Raunds.

Conference side Leek Town also faced a hectic end to the 1998 season – after losing 2–1 at home to Welling on 25 April, they drew 1–1 at Stevenage on the 27th. The next night at Slough the score was the same, before two days later they beat Yeovil 2–0 at home. Twenty-four hours afterwards they achieved a 2–2 draw with Morecambe before rounding off the season the following day with a 3–1 defeat at Hayes.

In the 1937–38 Northern League season, amateur side Bishop Auckland played their last 14 matches in 18 playing days, rising from third from bottom in the table to runners-up. The previous season saw them close their season with 18 games in 18 days.

FOOD

When 28-year-old Bosnian Muhammed Konjic signed for

Coventry in February 1999, he told them of a former transfer in 1995 when he was permitted to leave FC Sarajevo, while that city was under siege, to join NK Zagreb: 'I was sold for food. There was no point in paying cash because money did not mean anything – you could not buy anything.'

Sunderland fan Ron Thoms is hoping to cash in on the last meat pie sold at Roker Park in May 1997 before the stadium was demolished. Thirty-nine-year-old Navy officer Ron bought the pie and put it in the freezer to appreciate in value.

FOREIGNERS

Chelsea became the first League side to field a team made up entirely of non-British players on 26 December 1999 when they won 2–1 at Southampton in the Premiership. Their side was: De Goey (Netherlands), Ferrer (Spain), Thome (Brazil), Leboeuf (France), Babayaro (Nigeria), Petrescu (Romania), Deschamps (France), Di Matteo (Italy), Ambrosetti (Italy), Poyet (Uruguay), Flo (Norway). Said Italian boss Gianluca Vialli: 'We are an English side of English and foreign players. As long as we talk the same language on the pitch that's all that matters.'

Shortly after taking over as manager of Chelsea, Vialli demonstrated his grasp of English idioms in a post-match interview, when asked about his team's League and Cup form: 'At the start of the season, you're strong enough for both, but you must be as strong in March, when the fish are down.' I recently heard him describe football thus: 'As someone once said, it's an old, funny game.'

Belgium have conceded **fifty-six** goals in the final stages of World Cups.

Cheung Chi Doy was perhaps the first Chinese player in the English game, playing up front for Blackpool from 1960–62; while Egyptian H. Hegazi was Fulham's centre-forward during 1911–12.

Egyptian Tewfik Abdallah played 11 games for Hartlepool in the 1923–24 season.

Playing football was a potentially dangerous undertaking in Turkey at the turn of the 20th century, when it did not meet with the approval of the dictatorial government. Geoffrey Green, in his *Soccer The World Game*, reported that: 'In 1900 a group of Young Turks (a reference not to the age of those involved, but to a revolutionary movement) boldly took the game up and met at one of their leaders' houses to translate the English rules into Turkish.

'A palace spy heard of the meeting, entered the building with a detachment of soldiers and arrested the conspirators. His worst suspicions were confirmed when he discovered a pump, corner-post flags and multi-coloured shirts. In his report the shirts were described as uniforms, and the rules which the unlucky enthusiasts were translating as "proclamations". The football itself, which further search revealed, was called a "Top", which in Turkish means a cannon-ball. The offenders were banished, and the movement collapsed.'

GAS

Hard-up Romanian club Nitramonia Fagaras couldn't pay a £14,000 gas bill in summer 1999 – so they paid with two players who joined the state-run gas board's team.

GAY

Phoenix United Lesbian Club from Islington, North London, banned players from forming off-the-field relationships in June 1996 as past break-ups had led to players quitting the team.

'Nobody cares if Le Saux is gay or not. It is the fact that he openly admits to reading the *Guardian* that makes him the most reviled man in football.' Bizarre comment by *Daily Mirror* editor Piers Morgan about England defender Graeme Le Saux following his 1999 clash with Liverpool's Robbie Fowler, who made gestures at him with his hands and buttocks.

A number of clubs had British Rail LNER locomotives named in their honour during the 1930s. All had a prefix 28, with number **fifty-eight** designated as Newcastle United.

Gay magazine *Attitude* named its favourite footballers prior to the kick-off of the 1999–2000 season. Top of the list was David Beckham, described as having 'the face of an angel and the bum of a Greek god'.

GENITALS

The image of a ruthless Vinnie Jones grabbing the genital regions of a young Paul Gascoigne has been widely circulated. But a similar incident in 1943 nearly put England international and later Wolves boss, Stan Cullis, out of the game. During a match at Hampden in which England beat Scotland 4–0, Cullis recalled, 'I was standing in the wall when this big forward backed into me. Suddenly he reached behind him . . . and grabbed. I must have leapt two feet in the air. It was serious. I had to wear a special bandage for two years after that, from morning until night.'

GENIUS

'A floored genius.' Description of Duncan Ferguson in Everton's official 1998–99 yearbook.

GLASS

Christopher Daum, coach of German first division side Bayer Leverkusen, introduced a novel twist to training in July 1999 – making his players walk barefoot over glass. 'Willpower will win us the championship,' declared Daum, who had introduced an expert in positive thinking to his set-up.

After Courage Colts U14s took the lead in their April 1976 clash with Kent rivals Midas FC, things went downhill as they conceded **fifty-nine** goals in reply.

GOAL

Real Madrid were fined by UEFA after a goal collapsed before the start of their 1997–98 European Cup semi-final against Borussia Dortmund. Spectators had pulled at a hoarding to which it was attached – and it took over an hour to replace it.

Winger Reg Cutler hit the post for Bournemouth when the Third Division side played Wolves at Molineux in the FA Cup fourth round in the 1956–57 season. Unfortunately he did so literally – colliding with the post and knocking it over, causing the game to be delayed for repairs. Eventually the visitors knocked out their mighty hosts 1–0.

In August 1985 Newcastle defender Kenny Wharton suffered head and knee injuries – after being hit by a broken crossbar.

GOALKEEPERS

The first record of a club employing the desperate device of pushing their keeper upfield in a last-ditch attempt to score is contained in a contemporary report of the second FA Cup final, in which Wanderers beat Oxford University: 'The Oxonians, in the hopes of strengthening their attack, with questionable judgement determined on the removal of their goalkeeper. For a short time no disaster followed this ruse, but at length C.H. Wollaston, after a speedy run, reduced the Oxford goal by means of a neat kick with the left foot, thus placing the second goal to the credit of the Wanderers, entirely owing to the absence of the man between the posts.'

Stirling Albion had **sixty** points to aim at as a possible total in the 1954–55 Scottish League Division A season, but managed a record low of just six.

'I believe in Frankenstein, flying saucers and the hand of God. But most of all I believe in on-loan goalkeepers from Swindon scoring goals in the 95th minute.' Carlisle chairman Michael Knighton after his on-loan keeper Jimmy Glass scored to keep the side in the Third Division against Plymouth in May 1999.

It was said of pre-First World War Brighton keeper R. Whiting that he 'could kick a ball from his goal-line over the bar of the goal at the other end'.

Keepers J. Brownlie of Third Lanark and C. Hampton of Motherwell both scored when the two sides met in 1910.

Jack Kelsey, Welsh international goalkeeper of the 1950s, revealed the secret of his success: 'Chewing gum. Always use it. Put some on my hands. Rub it well in.'

GOAT

Whilst Watford were entertaining some unrecorded opponents at their Cassio Road ground during 1909 a goat encroached on to the pitch and, it was reported, 'in certain of its actions, spoke eloquently of its disgust for the whole dull and uneventful proceedings'. Some things never change.

GOD

Controversial faith healer Eileen Drewery, who was closely connected with the England camp during Glenn Hoddle's tenure as coach, claimed in April 1998 that she had asked God not to let Ian Wright score as time ran out in England's

Two hundred and **sixty-one** postponements due to bad weather made the 1962–63 FA Cup third round the longest ever staged in the competition, taking 66 days to complete.

1998 World Cup qualifier in Rome against Italy, which ended goalless. From close range, the normally lethal Wright hit the woodwork and Drewery later claimed: 'I had to send up a prayer: "Don't let him get a goal." It was so dangerous there.'

GUERILLAS

A team of Mexican guerillas, all clad in balaclavas to disguise their identity, played a 1999 match against a team of veteran former Mexican pros to gain publicity for their cause. Representing the Zapatista National Liberation Army and seeking to win support for Indian rights, some members of the team played the game at the Jesus Martin Palillo Stadium clad in army boots.

Frederick Ingram Walden, who died in 1949, was, at **sixty-two** inches tall, the shortest man ever to play for England.

HAIR

Turnstyles salon in Oxted, Surrey, claimed to be the world's first football barber's shop in March 1999 when hairdressers Tim Dodd and Rob Allbeury opened for business in a shop packed with football memorabilia. Arsenal fan Tim and Rob – who waters a precious piece of turf from his favourite team Brighton's old Goldstone Ground in the branch on a regular basis – cut hair whilst wearing replica kits. The salon also boasts seats from Chelsea's old West Stand.

Manchester United revealed during 1990 that promising youngster Chaz Hodges had refused to sign for them because they had demanded that he should have a haircut. 'I won't cut my hair for anyone except my mum,' he apparently replied – and vanished into oblivion.

Scotland coach Craig Brown used to appear in a rock 'n' roll group called Hammy and the Hamsters – sporting a quiff.

West Ham's Chilean player Javier Margas dyed his hair claret and blue for a UEFA Cup game against Osijek of Croatia in September 1999. Hammers won 3–0, prompting a *Daily Mirror* headline, 'Barnet 0 West Ham 3'.

When Romania beat England in the 1998 World Cup finals the whole of their team sported peroxide blond hair.

Newcastle and England's Steve Howey vainly decided to dye his greying hair in order to match the trendy barnets of his team-mates. However, he misread the instructions and ended up with a startling purple tint to his locks – which took until early 2000 to grow out.

HANDS

Taking on Rangers in the 1894 Scottish Cup semi-final, Queen's Park keeper Baird found himself in an awkward situation as the opposition attacked and David Boyd headed for goal. Baird was unable to save – as he'd caught his hand in the net.

Lazio defender Jose Antonio Chamot was sent off for shaking hands with referee Pierluigi Collina in April 1998, at the end of their 1–0 defeat by Juventus. Chamot was banned for one match after his handshake was construed as 'evident dissent'.

Northern Counties East League side Maltby Main boast probably the only one-handed keeper in the game – Darren Bonnington, who was born without a left hand and has just a little finger and a thumb.

Belgian player Joseph 'Jef' Jurion won **sixty-four** caps in the early sixties despite having to play wearing specially designed spectacles with unbreakable lenses, soft frames and rubber straps.

HEADS

Allistair Lang claimed a record in September 1998 when he scored with a header from 60 yards whilst playing for Northbank against Spittal Rovers in the Northern Alliance League. The FA told the 22-year-old that their records showed that the longest scoring header of which they were previously aware was scored from 35 yards by Peter Aldis for Aston Villa against Sunderland in 1952.

HEALER

Southampton striker Matt Le Tissier, often referred to as 'Le God' by fans, was credited with powers of healing by supporter Rebecca Malthouse in May 1998, after a wayward shot from the England international hit her hand as she sat behind the goal – and removed a fluid-filled ganglion, which was due to be operated on.

After Graham Taylor successfully took Watford into the Premiership via the play-offs at the end of the 1998–99 season, one of the secrets of his success was revealed by Wendy Thompson, wife of holistic healer Vincent John Thompson. Mrs Thompson told the *Guardian*: 'He took Graham Taylor up the mountain (Snowdon). He took him to an ancient church at the dead of night under the stars. He put him back together again.'

HEART

Italian Alessandro Pistone received a gift at the Newcastle players' Christmas party in 1998 – a sheep's heart wrapped in Xmas paper. He was told by an anonymous team-mate: 'It's because you haven't got a heart of your own.'

Former Feyenoord director Nicole Edelenbos was awarded **sixty-five** thousand pounds compensation in August 1998 after the club sacked her for dating Ajax manager Maarten Oldenhof.

Mansfield manager Steve Parkin was hooked up to a heart-rate monitor during the Sky transmission of his side's January 1999 Third Division clash with Rotherham. With 80 beats per minute normal and 120 rated cause for concern, Parkin's heart rate soared to 135, while that of his opposite number, Ronnie Moore, stayed steady at 85. But then Rotherham did win.

HELMETS

Roma turned out for a Serie A fixture against Cagliari in 1999 wearing crash helmets – to publicise a police motorbike safety drive.

HIGH JUMP

Keeper Ben Howard Baker, who joined Chelsea in 1921, boasted of being world high jump record holder.

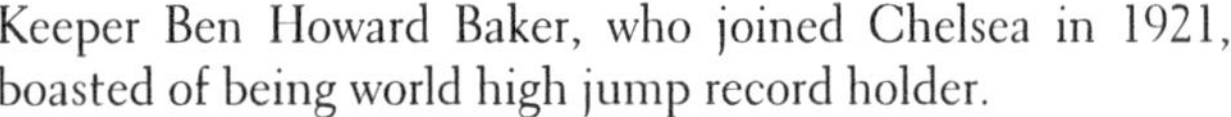

HOAX

The *News of the World*, *The Times* and the Liverpool ClubCall telephone line all agreed that the Anfield side were keen to snap up £3.5m French World Cup star Didier Baptiste in November 1999 – until someone pointed out that although there was a star player called Didier Baptiste, he was a fictional character in the Sky TV football soap opera *Dream Team*. It transpired that no one had taken the trouble to check out an Internet story put out by a hoaxer.

Mickleover Lightning Blue Sox beat Chellaston Boys B in the Derby Under-10s Community Cup in December 1998 after a penalty shoot-out lasting a record **sixty-six** kicks, only three of which were converted.

HOMESICK

Having played for Chelsea for five years up to 1991, striker Gordon Durie announced he was homesick for his native Scotland – and signed for Spurs.

ICE

Halifax Town discovered a novel way of increasing their income during the big freeze of winter 1963 – they opened their ground to the public as an ice rink.

Manchester United swooped for Stockport County wing-half Hughie McLenahan in 1927, snapping him up for a payment of three freezers of ice cream – which was subsequently sold to raise funds at the club bazaar.

ICON

'His use of the English language, especially in his football reporting, has made him an icon with the youth of today. His mellifluous voice is redolent of Sinden and Gielgud intertwining Shakespeare, Keats, Wordsworth et al amid the mud and tears at Accrington Stanley.' A tribute to Radio 5 Live commentator Stuart Hall from a motion tabled in the House of Commons in February 1999 by Labour MP Tom Pendry and Tory David Ruffley.

Liverpool set a First Division record for points won (before three for a win) with **sixty-eight** from 42 games in 1978–79.

ILLNESS

Doctors in Florence identified an illness which they dubbed 'Mal di Fiorentina' in November 1999 after Professors Pierluigi Cabras, director of Florence's clinic of psychology, and Franco Pacini, chief physician of gastroenterology at a Florence hospital, discovered that 'the illness was caused by the stress of supporting Fiorentina'.

IMPLANTS

Former Leeds and Crystal Palace player Tomas Brolin of Sweden issued a single during 1999, 'Alla Vi', the video for which was barred in his native country for featuring 'too many breast implants and too few clothes'. Nonetheless it hit the Swedish top 20.

INJURY

Arrangements for injured players have not always been sophisticated. When Arsenal's George Jobey was injured during a 1913 match against Leicester Fosse, 'trainer George Hardy had to borrow a milk cart from David Lewis, a dairyman in Gillespie Road, to wheel Jobey to his lodgings'.

Bert Trautmann, Manchester City's German goalkeeper, played on until the end of the 1956 FA Cup final despite having broken his neck whilst making a save during the match.

Torquay chairman Mervyn Benny banned his players from pre-match shooting practice during the 1998–99 season as he feared their wayward shooting could injure fans behind the

A crowd of eighteen thousand and **sixty-nine** turned up to see Wrexham Reserves play Wisford United in January 1957 – because tickets were on sale for a Cup game against Manchester United.

goals. The club had already had to pay compensation to a woman whose glasses had been broken, while scores of seats had been damaged by stray shots. Mr Benny took the action when he heard of a Huddersfield fan who planned to sue after her arm was broken at a match.

'Waste him!' – two words which won $277,000 in damages for Piper High School player Gary Beharrie, who needed knee surgery after an opponent intentionally injured him in 1992. Coach Phil Droskick of Deerfield Beach High admitted yelling the instruction to one of his players.

Doctors at Wexham Park Hospital in Slough reported the first cases of virtual football injuries in November 1999. Players of an arcade football game wear helmets which immerse them in what appears to be a real match; a sensor attached to their foot is the ball. Orthopaedic registrar Graham Tytherleigh-Strong reported: 'One patient kicked the ball so hard he fell off the game table and broke his ankle; another fractured two toes on his right foot when he kicked the bars on the table attempting an ambitious shot.'

In 1975 Manchester United keeper Alex Stepney screamed so hard at his defenders that he broke his jaw.

David Batty aggravated an Achilles tendon injury whilst at Newcastle when his toddler rode his tricycle into the back of Batty's legs.

Charlie George of Arsenal cut his big toe off with a lawnmower.

Seventy-year-old Billy McPhail, a former Celtic player, lost a Social Security case to prove that his pre-senile dementia memory loss had been caused by heading old-time leather footballs.

Allan Nielsen of Spurs missed several matches after his daughter poked him in the eye with her fingers.

WBA striker Lee Hughes was knocked unconscious after slipping on an ice cube in December 1998.

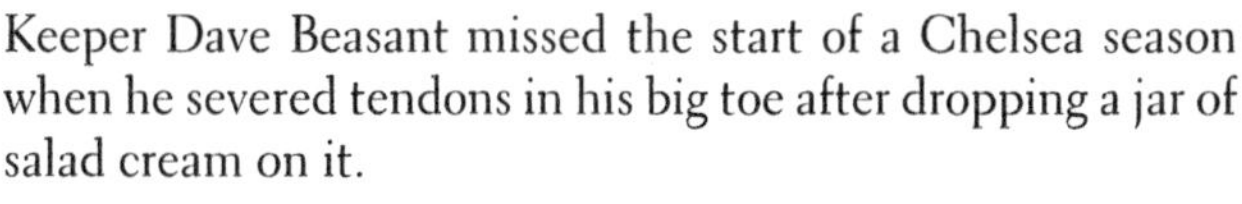

Keeper Dave Beasant missed the start of a Chelsea season when he severed tendons in his big toe after dropping a jar of salad cream on it.

Coventry striker Robbie Keane had to have a knee operation after bending down to pick up the remote control for his TV.

Former Spurs and England defender Alan Mullery once missed out on a cap when he cricked his neck whilst shaving.

Noel Whelan of Coventry was out for half a season after putting his ankle through a plate glass window.

Danish keeper Michael Stensgaard's career at Liverpool was curtailed in the mid-1990s when he injured his shoulder whilst trying to prevent an ironing board from falling over.

INTERNET

Prestigious American magazine *Time* ran a poll to discover the most influential person of the 20th century – and were a little surprised when obscure Irish footballer Ronnie O'Brien stormed to an overwhelming lead in the voting. *Time* had run its 1999 poll on the Internet and e-mail jokers encouraged

Between 1977 and 1990, Frank Stapleton scored 20 goals in **seventy-one** games for the Republic of Ireland.

Irish Internet enthusiasts to vote for the 20-year-old player, who was released by Middlesbrough but signed by Juventus. Their scheme was so successful that *Time*'s website crashed under the volume of votes for O'Brien.

Leeds United's appearance record is held by Jack Charlton, who turned out for them seven hundred and **seventy-two** times between 1952 and 1973.

JAIL

Jason Snaith, 24, of Creasey Park Social FC became the first player known to have taken part in a match whilst wearing an electronic tracking tag in November 1999. Snaith was released after serving half of an assault sentence but had to wear the tag to ensure he observed a curfew. He helped team-mates to a 1–1 draw against Mulberry Bush in a Leighton Buzzard, Beds. league.

Linesman Neil Bassford got a two-month suspended jail term and a fine in October 1997 after storming on to the pitch as Birstall United and Ratby Sports fought out a Leicester Sunday League game and assaulting two Ratby players with his flag.

1980s Chelsea keeper, Yugoslav Petar Borota, was jailed in Belgrade for his part in a stolen picture racket.

Arsenal and England player Ray Parlour was arrested and thrown in jail in Hong Kong in 1995 for throwing Chinese

Two hundred and **seventy-three** clubs playing in Paris's Seine-Saint-Denis area were suspended in April 1999 after 800 cases of violence in March alone.

crackers at a taxi driver following a 12-pint binge.

Two prisoners escaped from Sarajevo jail in Bosnia as warders watched the 1999 European Cup final. Both were armed robbers serving 20 years.

Tony Adams of Arsenal and England was jailed for four months for drink-driving in December 1990.

Thomas McGowan, 22, was jailed for five months in June 1999 after posing as Celtic's Henrik Larsson in order to use the striker's stolen credit card.

Former Northampton Town footballer Chad Bone, 27, scored a spectacular own goal when, in June 1999, he tried to have a three-month jail sentence for attacking a girlfriend overturned. Instead he was given six months by a Newcastle upon Tyne judge.

Graham Allner, manager of Dr Martens League side Worcester City, signed 29-year-old Darren Steadman during season 1998–99, even though Steadman was serving a two-year jail sentence, with one year suspended, in Grange Prison near Redditch – for a mortgage swindle. Under a resettlement scheme for offenders, Steadman was allowed out to play for Worcester.

In 1971 a South American Club Cup game in Buenos Aires between Boca Juniors and Peru's Sporting Cristal became so violent that both sets of players were locked up in prison and only released the next day.

Cambridge United and Oldham drew 2–2 on 6 January nineteen **seventy-four** in the first FA Cup match ever played on a Sunday.

Czech football fan Edouard Kareil was jailed for a month in Prague in April 1997 after forcing his 27-year-old wife, Christer, to sleep with a player who scored for the team he supports. He said he'd done it as an incentive for the side.

Vasile Ianul, former head of Dinamo Bucharest, was sentenced to 12 years in jail in May 1999 after a military court found him guilty of embezzling over £1.6m during his spell as club president from 1991–94.

President Ongania of Argentina imprisoned four members of the Estudiantes team after the second leg of their World Club Cup final against Milan descended into violence. One of the players, keeper Pierino Prati, who had kicked an injured Milan player in the back while he lay on the pitch, was banned for life.

Ken Richardson, former owner of Doncaster Rovers, was jailed in March 1999 for four years for plotting to burn down the club's main stand.

Drawn against Southampton St Mary's in the FA Cup of 1894, Reading were keen to play their forward Jimmy Stewart, a private in the King's Own Regiment, who happened to be in detention in the guardroom for a breach of discipline. Reading secretary Horace Walker bribed Stewart's guards with bottles of Scotch and secured permission for the jailbird to play in the match – in which he scored the winner before returning to complete his jankers.

A football fan was jailed in February 1999 for two months in Reims, France, after he stopped the opposition scoring by shooting a goalbound ball with his revolver.

During season 1958–59, Lincoln City boasted a defender called Ray Long who was **seventy-five** inches tall and a striker Joe Short who was 5ft 2ins.

KIT

'Forget suspenders and sexy lingerie,' said Sky TV's *Soccer AM* presenter and Torquay fan Helen Chamberlain in December 1998: 'What you need is to get your kit on and get down to it. I make my boyfriend wear the Torquay away kit – I just love the noise two football tops make when they rub together. It's a real turn-on.'

Beaten by Cardiff in the 1927 FA Cup final, Arsenal claimed that their defeat was due to the brand new jersey worn by keeper Dan Lewis, which enabled the wet ball to wriggle under his body for the decisive goal. For years afterwards they insisted that their keepers should only wear previously washed jerseys.

Striker Tony Cascarino, who went on to win over 50 caps for the Republic of Ireland, was signed from non-league Crockenhill by Gillingham for a team kit.

Hard-up Portsmouth had to take drastic steps to save money when the club went into administration in the 1998–99 season – so they cancelled their weekly order of new jockstraps for players, saving £112. Said administrator Tom Burton: 'We were having new jockstraps for every game, so I said why not wash the damn things?'

KNICKERS

Spanish side Bejar Industrial were struggling at the foot of their table in April 1999, so in an effort to improve their fortunes, four of their players wore knickers belonging to wives and girlfriends and adorned with the club badge during their match against Zamora, which they won 1–0. The rest of the team followed suit for the next match – but the knickers went down to a 2–1 defeat.

After struggling all season in Bedfordshire Leighton & District Sunday League, Edlesborough FC suddenly hit a winning streak when midfielder Jamie Mitchell had to turn out wearing a girlfriend's knickers, after forgetting to bring his pants. After that the rest of his team-mates began to follow suit, and the side moved up the table as they played in bras, leotards and French knickers. Commented a league official in December 1998: 'There is no rule against the wearing of knickers and basques.'

LAMP

Huddersfield might have rubbed FA Cup final opponents Aston Villa up the wrong way prior to the 1920 showdown, when they brought into their dressing room a lamp from a local pantomime production of *Aladdin*. All the players rubbed the lamp for luck before they went out – to lose 1–0.

LAWNMOWER

Whilst boss at non-league Kettering Town, Ron Atkinson didn't have much money to splash out on transfers, but was active in the market nonetheless: 'Once we swapped one of our players for a lawnmower. We got the best out of that deal. The player lasted about ten games for the club and we got eight or nine years' service out of the mower.'

LEGS

'What he's got is legs, which is different from the other midfielders we've got.' Lennie Lawrence, then manager of

The referee's whistle was introduced to the game in eighteen **seventy-eight** – the first recorded occasion being a game between Nottingham Forest and Sheffield Norfolk.

Luton Town, discusses star of the future Matthew Spring during 1998, in the process highlighting the reason the club has failed to set the Second Division alight in recent seasons.

Confident of victory in their North Cup final at Maine Road in 1945, Manchester United paraded a one-legged man hopping around in a red singlet and white shorts before kick-off to symbolise the fact that they could beat Bolton on one leg. They didn't, though, Wanderers coming out on top.

'In Cameroon, healers have said they will be able to cure me in three days by burying my leg in the ground and putting fire around it. They have also recommended massage with gorilla bones while invoking the spirits of ancestors. Physiotherapy would include going on a hedgehog hunt.' Reported comments of West Ham's Cameroon midfielder Marc-Vivien Foe on possible treatment for a broken leg sustained at the 1998 World Cup finals.

LIGHTS

A spate of floodlight failures at high-profile matches in 1997–98 led to rumours of interference by Far Eastern betting syndicates who, allegedly, stood to benefit by having their bets settled at the score prevailing when the lights went out.

The first match at Derby's new Pride Park in August 1997 was abandoned after 56 minutes when the lights went out with the home side 2–1 up against Wimbledon. In November of the same year the Premiership match between West Ham and Crystal Palace at Upton Park was abandoned after 65 minutes at 2–2. The next month it happened for a third time when Wimbledon v Arsenal at Selhurst Park was abandoned at 0–0 immediately after the start of the second half.

Derek Possee's club record of **seventy-nine** goals for Millwall was beaten on 16 February, 1991 when Teddy Sheringham scored all four goals as the Lions beat Plymouth 4–1. Teddy was also scoring the 3200th Football League goal of the season and equalled John Calvey's Millwall record of 89 League and Cup goals, achieved a century earlier.

A day later the police announced they would be investigating claims of betting syndicate involvement. Subsequently a number of men were arrested in connection with an attempt to interfere with the floodlights at Charlton's ground.

LINESMEN

Dutch scientist Dr Raoul Oudejans and a group of colleagues published research in *Nature* magazine in February 2000 indicating that, wait for it, up to one in five offside decisions by linesmen are inaccurate.

Their ground-breaking research, carried out by a Vrije University of Amsterdam team, involved multi-camera analysis of 200 decisions which were then re-adjudicated by three professional linesmen.

Explaining their apparently pointless work, the good doctor commented: 'The assistant referee cannot see passer and receiver simultaneously. This causes him to shift his gaze from passer to receiver and so make judgements a split second after the moment of passing – long enough for the receiver to have gone past the last defender and to appear offside.'

LOTTERY

When the residents of southern Italian village Peschici won £23 million in a lottery in November 1998 they put in an offer for Ronaldo to sign up for their local side. Inter Milan turned down the bid.

Manchester City, who scored **eighty** goals, three more than champions Arsenal, were relegated in 1938, having started the season as reigning champions.

LOYALTY

Fanatical Portsmouth fan John Portsmouth Football Club Westwood, who changed his name by deed poll, was presented with a long-service loyalty award by the club prior to their December 1998 match against Grimsby. Sadly he was banned for life from the ground after running on to the pitch after the game.

Darren Beeley takes a 700-mile round trip from his home in Fort William, Scotland, to watch every Rotherham United home game. The 27-year-old travelled 1,300 miles when his side lost at Plymouth in 1999.

Sixty-year-old Newcastle fan granny Beryl Owen made a 550-mile trip from her Holyhead home to St James's Park on a regular basis during the 1998–99 season, just to stand outside the ground to listen to matches as she couldn't get tickets.

Forty-six-year-old John Brooke was kidnapped at gunpoint in the Yemen and held by terrorists for four days in January 1999. As soon as he was freed he requested to make an urgent phone call – to find out how Norwich City had got on in their latest match. Wife Katherine, 45, was able to tell him the bad news – they had squandered a two-goal lead to lose 3–2.

Gillingham fan Kevin Champ flew from Adelaide to watch his favourite side take on Manchester City in the Division Two play-off final at Wembley in May 1999. The 49-year-old saw his side two goals up with a minute to go, only to lose on penalties after City scored twice in ordinary and injury time. He then flew straight back.

Eighty-one-year-old Matt Clark accepted a £750,000 cheque from Vernons Pools in August 1993 – having had a practice run in 1969 when he won £778,426 from them.

A man from Leeds won a brewery-sponsored competition in January 1999 offering the chance to visit any football stadium in the world to see a match. He chose to visit Elland Road, Leeds.

Soccer writer Hunter Davies has season tickets for both Arsenal and Spurs. He explained in June 1998: 'I go to see Spurs win and Arsenal stuffed.' He was less keen on this explanation in 1999 when he was recognised by an Arsenal fan who recalled his alternative 'loyalty' and bopped him on the nose.

In nineteen **eighty-two** Chesterfield's Geoff Salmons voluntarily sacrificed his wages when he was ruled out of action for three weeks with a hamstring injury.

MAGIC

During a vital African Champions League match between Ferroviario of Mozambique and Dynamo of Zimbabwe, a player from the former side snatched the gloves from the Dynamo keeper who had made a string of saves, and waved them around in an effort, he later explained, to shake out the magic spirits which were protecting his goal. After this incident, declared a 1998 report, the pitch was invaded and a riot ensued which resulted in Mozambique having to make an official apology for the conduct of the fans. Dynamo won 1–0.

MANAGER

Spanish second division striker Sabino Santos, of Badajoz, burst clear and bore down on the Leganes goal, only to be foiled by a last-ditch tackle – by the opposition manager, Enrique Martin, who rushed on to the pitch to haul the attacker down. After receiving a ten-match ban in November 1999, Martin tried to defend his actions by claiming he believed Santos was offside.

Willy van der Kerkhof scored after **eighty-three** minutes for Holland against Austria in the 1978 World Cup finals. In the next game his twin Rene scored – after 83 minutes.

MARRIAGE

'Man offers marriage to woman supplying Cup final ticket for next Saturday's game. Replies must enclose photograph of ticket.' Advert from the Personal columns of *The Times*, prior to the 1950 FA Cup final between Arsenal and Liverpool.

Doncaster Rovers fan Graham Mills went to watch them play Northampton in September 1995. Rovers won – but 45-year-old Graham was a loser, when his ex-wife accepted a proposal of marriage from her secret lover on the pitch at half-time. Over 2,000 fans heard Doncaster's community coach and former Sunderland player John Mounsey, 42, ask for 27-year-old Tracey's hand during the interval. And she said yes.

Said Graham, 'We had split up, but I'd no idea anything like this was going to happen.'

MASCOTS

Supporters of French first division side St Etienne chose an unusual club mascot for their team in 1999–2000 – the 2,000-strong 'Magic Fans' chose porn star Elodie Cherie, who claims to have supported the club since the age of six.

FC Zurich have as their mascot a bull named Maradona.

Wycombe introduced assistant manager Terry Gibson's new signing at their official photograph session prior to the 1999–2000 season – a five-foot wooden Indian chief.

Writer Rogan Taylor, who attended the 1998 African

England took three hundred and **eighty-four** Mars bars with them to the 1986 World Cup finals.

Nations Cup, described host nation Burkina Faso's mascot: 'A guy dressed up in a policeman's jacket, two ties around his neck, a pleated skirt, odd socks and a pair of joke tits and bum balloons. He carried a golf umbrella, wore shades with one eyeglass missing and a white dunce's hat.'

Albert Lambert was a mascot for his local side, South Shields, when four years old in 1911. Eighty years later he performed the same function for Slough Town before their Conference match against Gateshead.

Toby the (real) Sheep, mascot for Greenock Morton before the First World War, was left in the changing room after a winning match – only to drown in the players' bath.

Barnsley mascot Toby Tyke, a cavorting seven-foot bulldog, provoked outrage amongst Manchester City fans on Boxing Day 1996 when he cocked his leg at visiting supporters.

A half-time punch-up flared between mascots at a 1998 match between Bristol City and Wolves. One of three Coldseal Pigs, there to promote a double-glazing firm, swung a trotter at the visitors' Wolfie, while City Cat also became involved and stewards had to intervene. 'Wolfie told me to f*** off' alleged Paddy Kelly, alias a Coldseal Pig, who in turn accused Wolfie of shoving over a fellow porker. Avon & Somerset police commented: 'We understand there was a lot of huffing and puffing.'

Dundee United's 7ft 2in Terry the Terror lion kicked TV commentator Chick Young, himself wearing a Santa suit, during an It's a Knockout competition in Glasgow. Young

Chelsea's disciplinary record for season 1998–99 was the second worst in the Premiership with **eighty-five** yellow cards, four red, committing 548 fouls.

was left concussed during a penalty shoot-out between rival mascots, but Terry the Terror claimed, 'The costume slipped over my eyes and I couldn't tell what was the ball and what was Chick.'

Wolfie of Wolves was in trouble again in early 1999 after allegedly attacking Baggie Bird, WBA's mascot, at Molineux. He was reported to the FA by Albion fan Noel Bishop who said, 'His behaviour could have sparked off serious crowd trouble.'

Sammy the Seagull of Scarborough had the bare-faced cheek to 'moon' at rival fans during a game against Brentford in September 1998.

Cambridge United's Marvin the Moose was warned about his behaviour after 'encouraging – by use of a rapid moose-hoof gesture – the fans to speculate about the referee's favourite solo hobby'.

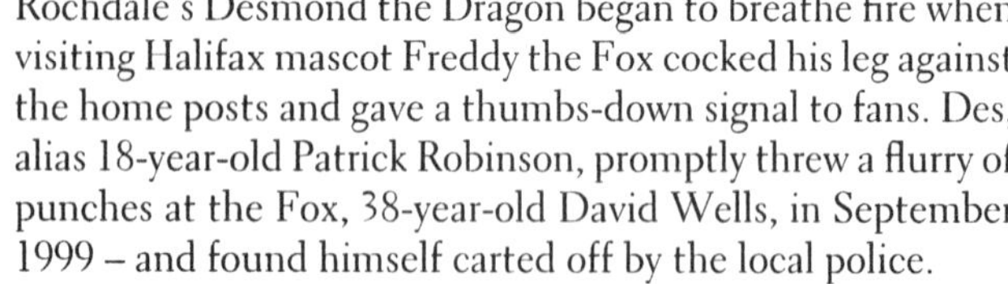

Rochdale's Desmond the Dragon began to breathe fire when visiting Halifax mascot Freddy the Fox cocked his leg against the home posts and gave a thumbs-down signal to fans. Des, alias 18-year-old Patrick Robinson, promptly threw a flurry of punches at the Fox, 38-year-old David Wells, in September 1999 – and found himself carted off by the local police.

Tranmere Rovers' Terrier was reprimanded by club officials in December 1998 after being caught swinging on the nets and cocking his leg up against the goalposts.

Prince Albert became the first member of the Royal Family to visit a football match when, in October eighteen **eighty-six**, he went to Turf Moor to see Burnley playing Bolton.

Nine-foot-tall Cyril the Swan, Swansea City's mascot, made history as the first swan to be charged with bringing the game into disrepute after running on to the pitch to join in goal celebrations in February 1999, when Swansea scored against Millwall in the FA Cup. Referee Steve Dunn took a dim view of the incursion and reported the incident. Cyril, who turned up in person at the April 1999 hearing, earned his club a £1,000 fine from the Welsh FA, who banned him from the touchline while players are on the pitch. Previously, both Cyril and Cardiff's Barclay the Bluebird had been barred from a November 1998 clash between the two Welsh sides for fear of triggering violence.

1999 was altogether an eventful year for Cyril. When Swansea were narrowly defeated by Premiership side Derby in January, the *Sun* awarded him their Man of the Match accolade. He was later banned from being nominated for the BBC TV Welsh Sports Personality of the Year award on the grounds that he was not real – but objections from angry Swansea fans resulted in a climbdown from officials who finally allowed him to take part.

Cyril, whose identity remains secret, released his anthem, 'Nice Swan Cyril', on CD, selling 2,000 copies, and was invited to make the National Lottery draw.

MEAT

Romanian paper *Evenimentul Zilei* reported in March 1998 that the bottom team in their first division, Jiul Petrosani, had sold midfielder Ion Radu to second division Vilcea for 1,200 lb of meat.

MEDALS

J. Delaney created a unique record when he won Scottish (Celtic, 1937), English (Manchester United, 1948),

Northern Irish (Derry City, 1954) and Eire (Cork Athletic, 1956) Cup medals.

MILLENNIUM

Chertsey of Ryman League Division One found themselves the holders of two distinctions on 30 December 1999, when they entertained Bishop's Stortford in one of the final senior matches played on the British mainland in the 20th century. They lost 5–3 but their midfielder Rob French scored the last senior goal of the millennium and Ryan Ashe was the last player sent off in a senior game.

MISSING LIMB

Keeper Rudi Hiden played 20 times for Austria from May 1928 before moving to play in France and becoming naturalised to that country. Returning to Vienna, Hiden sadly had a leg amputated in 1968, but was refused a state pension by Austria on the grounds that he was a 'foreigner'.

Hungarian international keeper Karoly Zsak continued to play for his country until 1925, winning 30 caps, despite having a finger amputated in the early 20s.

MOLE

The referee of a South African Premier League match stopped play during the November 1999 clash between Mother City and Classic of Tembissa in Cape Town – because a mole had taken up position in one of the goalmouths and was refusing to leave. The mole was coaxed on to a stretcher and carried off.

An eighteen **eighty-eight** game between Scottish FA Cup winners Renton and their English equivalents, West Bromwich, was billed as a contest for the 'Championship of the World'.

MUSIC

A Texan rock band named themselves after Port Vale, having come across the club's name on the Internet during 1999.

'Cole raps pretty much the way he talks – and if you've ever heard him talk you really don't want to hear him rap.' *Telegraph*'s Neil McCormick on Andy Cole's 1999 debut single, 'Outstanding'.

Accompanying Arsenal to Wembley for the FA Cup final against Manchester United in 1979, journalist Martin Tyler was intrigued to hear records by Max Bygraves being played on the coach's sound system. He was told: 'We play Max Bygraves on the way to matches as an incentive. If we lose we have to listen to it on the way back!' Arsenal lost.

German international Oliver Bierhoff trained as an opera singer.

Bobby Gould realised his time as manager of Wales was coming to an end in 1998 when the Manic Street Preachers rock band began campaigning against him – even changing the lyrics of one of their songs to anti-Gould sentiments. He finally went in June 1999.

We all know those terrible old football songs like 'Blue Is The Colour' and 'Good Old Arsenal', but ever so occasionally respectable artistes include reference to the beautiful game in their lesser-known tracks.

Like Squeeze, on their 1995 *Ridiculous* album, who, on the track 'Walk Away', sing: 'A black and white photograph

Having become Leeds' youngest-ever player in September 1962, aged 15 years and two hundred and **eighty-nine** days, Peter Lorimer became their oldest some time later, aged 38 years 17 days.

of me up the garden path wrapped up in my football scarf . . .' And Paul McCartney, whose 1997 *Flaming Pie* contained a track called 'Somedays' in which the great man declares, 'It's no good asking me . . . who won the match or scored the goal . . .'

A group of Sunderland fans brought out a 1999 single called 'Niall Quinn's Disco Pants'.

Former US World Cup star Alexei Lalas brought out a well-received rock album in 1998.

Sunderland amassed **ninety** points in the 1997–98 First Division season – the greatest number ever obtained by a side failing to win promotion.

NAKED

Paulo Mata, coach of Brazilian side Itaperuna, ran on to the pitch, dropped his trousers and mooned at the referee after his side went down 3–2 to a late goal which he considered to be offside in March 1997. 'I went naked because I'm tired of working honestly only to be scandalously robbed,' he claimed.

Non-league Romanian side Athletic Bucharest were fined £10,000 by the Romanian Football Federation after failing to finish a game which they had been losing 16–0. The side claimed that they left the pitch with two minutes remaining after unruly gypsy fans threatened 'to strip them naked if they conceded two more goals', according to the *Evenimentul Zilei* newspaper in October 1996.

Scunthorpe manager Brian Laws asked Nottingham Forest striker Steve Guinan in November 1999 whether he wanted to extend his loan spell at the club. When the player declined, Laws told him to leave the club immediately and

Collecting **ninety-one** yellow cards, five dismissals, and committing 587 fouls, Everton had the worst 1998–99 Premiership disciplinary record.

ordered him to remove his club tracksuit – leaving him standing 'half naked' in the club car park. 'I only want players who want to play for Scunthorpe wearing our tracksuits,' declared the unrepentant Laws.

Norway's leading club Rosenborg announced in June 1999 that it was banning female journalists from changing rooms, despite having traditionally allowed them free access to conduct interviews. 'The fact is we don't want female reporters in the changing room. I'm married and the only woman allowed to see me naked is my wife,' said a surprisingly modest-sounding club captain, Jahn Ivar Jakobsen.

Reporter Mari By-Rise of the *Dagbladet* newspaper riposted, 'When I'm working I have neither the time nor the desire to study what the boys look like without clothes.'

Leicester City's magazine ran a photograph of Muzzy Izzet, naked but for a strategically placed football, in November 1996 and jokingly offered uncensored versions for sale. 'We had 30 calls in the first hour of going on sale,' said editor Paul Mace.

Spurs and England keeper Ian Walker once earned a reported £10,000 for posing naked in *For Women* magazine.

Eager to persuade his players to train despite a snow-covered pitch, Hartlepool's Bill Norman, manager from 1927–31, 'showed them what could be done by taking off all his clothes and rolling in the snow'.

After Conference side Hereford beat York in the FA Cup first round, thanks to a goal by Leroy May, the striker revealed

When Dutchman Eric van Dorp visited Darlington's ground in April 1999, he became the first non-British resident to have visited all **ninety-two** professional football grounds in England and Wales.

that he boosted his earnings by £500 a week by appearing as a male stripper with, he claimed, the full support of his wife.

Luther College in Decorah, Iowa, banned its traditional naked football match to mark the end of school exams in May 1998, after the previous year's mixed-sex game resulted in seven students being charged with indecent exposure.

NAME GAME

The Scottish referee on the 1958 World Cup panel was Edward Charles Faultless.

Shaka Hislop changed his name from Neil, in honour of the king of the Zulus. He also went to school with Brian Lara and became a robotics engineer with NASA.

A little-known honour for striker Chris Sutton emerged in late 1999 when a Microsoft survey revealed that his surname graced 321 Avenues, Roads, Rows, Streets etc. in the country – over three times more than the surname of any other England player.

TV commentators were a little wary of the names of a number of Euro 96 players which may have been open to dual interpretation. Stefan Kuntz of Germany was a particular problem, as were Russia's Nikersov and Khokhlov, while they had to take care with Dutchman de Kock and Bulgaria's Yankov.

Chelsea's 1958 European Fairs Cup opponents, Frem

Denmark boasts a club called B.**ninety-three** – not to be confused with another, named B.1903.

Copenhagen, boasted a keeper called Bent Koch.

Celtic officials were worried that rival fans might taunt their new Brazilian signing if they put his last name on the back of his shirt when they signed him in late 1999, so they called him Rafael – instead of Scheidt. Just as well they hadn't also signed Spanish star Turdo.

Spurs' White Hart Lane ground may not have had the same ring to it had the original wishes of the club to christen it 'Percy Park' been accepted.

Asked where he got the nickname 'Chief' from, Wimbledon striker Efan Ekoku revealed: 'My dad's been a chief since 1973 in a town called Agbor, Nigeria.'

Dennis Bergkamp's father wanted to name him Denis, in tribute to Denis Law – but the Dutch registrar refused to accept that spelling, saying it was too similar to Denise.

Arsenal's legendary manager Herbert Chapman persuaded London Transport to rename their Gillespie Road underground station Arsenal.

Winger Mark Walters moved from Rangers to Liverpool in 1991, despite the fact that his middle name is Everton.

Most people know why they acquire a nickname, but not the man with possibly the best known nickname of all – Edson Arantes do Nascimento, better known as Pele, who declares:

A colour poster measuring **ninety-four** by 71cm of Pelé, autographed in green chalk, was sold at an auction in 1998 for £450.

'I have no idea where it came from or who started it. The name Pele has no meaning in Portuguese or any other language as far as I am aware.'

The Australian keeper who was humiliated in 1951 when they were beaten 17–0 by an English FA touring XI was called Conquest. First name? Norman.

Proud mother Diane Waterfield, 31, from Margate in Kent, named her newly born daughter Manchester in October 1999, as her entire family are United fans.

Manchester United fan Jason Villette, from Finedon, Northants, called his three sons Ince, Cantona and, in September 1999, Beckham.

Supporter Dave Tolley of Kidderminster named his newly born son Tyler Birmingham City Tolley in February 1999.

Dairy worker Michael Faulder, 35, of Ashchurch, Glos., christened his son Michael Owen Anfield Shankly Faulder.

Newcastle fans Fiona and Paul Dixon from County Durham called their children Keegan, Beardsley and Dalglish – the latter two are girls.

Cardiff fan Graham Hall, 22, celebrated his club's promotion to Division Two in 1999 by changing his name by deed poll to that of his favourite player, Kevin Nugent.

A survey before the 1998 World Cup revealed that **ninety-five** per cent of men aged 20 to 34 would prefer to watch a soccer match on TV rather than enjoy a romp with a supermodel.

Lifelong Liverpool fan Duncan Oldham, 24, was reported to have changed his name by deed poll to Manchester United in June 1999 to raise cash for a hospice in Scarborough.

The *Guardian* reported in 1997 that Doncaster football fan Kelvin Pratt was so fed up with people making fun of his name that he had decided to change it . . . to Paul Gascoigne.

Coming on as sub for France against Germany during the 1986 World Cup, Daniel Xuereb completed the alphabet of World Cup players – every other initial letter had already been represented.

Avante Garde were winners of the Tunisian League in 1928, and its Cup in 1922.
Cape Coast Dwarfs won the Ghanaian League in 1968 and their Cup in 1969.

Diables Noirs have several Congolese League and Cup triumphs to their name.
Eleven Wise FC were 1982 Ghanaian Cup winners.
Liverpool were 1965 League champions in Kenya.
Arsenal were 1989 and 1991 Cup winners in Lesotho.
Invincible Eleven almost lived up to their name by winning the Liberian League eight times between 1965 and 1987.
FC Dodo proved they were far from extinct by winning the Mauritius League title in 1970.

Sunshine were champions of Seychelles in 1995.
Mighty Blackpool FC walked off with the championship of Sierra Leone from 1994–97.
Wankie landed the Zimbabwean Cup in 1970, and again in 1992.
Violent Kickers hopefully did not live up to their name in winning the Jamaican League title in 1994 and 1996.
Robin Hood have been a dominant force in the Surinam

Premiership clubs paid out a total of two hundred and **ninety-six** million pounds in wages to players in season 1997–98.

League for over 40 years, claiming 22 titles between 1952 and 1994.

The early names of some famous old clubs give a clear indication of their origins – while others are a little more obscure:

Bolton Wanderers . . . Christ Church Sunday School FC
Bristol Rovers . . . Black Arabs
Gillingham . . . New Brompton Excelsior
Motherwell . . . Wee Alpha
Oldham Athletic . . . Pine Villa
Queen's Park Rangers . . . St Jude's Institute
Stockport County . . . Heaton Norris

Betting on Premiership football is very popular with Far Eastern punters – shady illegal syndicates or not! – and a recent article in the *Observer* revealed the way in which Cantonese-speaking punters indicate which team they wish to bet on:

Arsenal . . . Ah Sin No
Aston Villa . . . Ah Shi Ton Wai Lai
Blackburn Rovers . . . Poeh Lik Pun Lau Lorng
Charlton . . . Cha Yi Tun
Chelsea . . . Chea Lo Si
Coventry . . . Koeh Wan Tei Ley
Derby County . . . Tah Pei Gan
Everton . . . Oi Wah Tun
Leeds United . . . Lik Si Luen

Leicester City . . . Lei Si Tat Sing
Liverpool . . . Lei Mut Poh
Manchester United . . . Marn Luen
Middlesbrough . . . Mei Toeh Si Poeh
Newcastle . . . Ngau Kah So
Nottingham Forest . . . Lok Ting Ham Su Lam
Sheffield Wed . . . Sek Chou Sam

Pelé scored a record **ninety-seven** goals in full internationals between 1957–70.

Southampton . . . Sau Ham Tun
Tottenham Hotspur . . . Yit Chi
West Ham . . . Wa Si Ham
Wimbledon . . . One Poeh Tun.

Fred Blackadder was a centre-half who played for Carlisle in Division Three North during the 1946–47 season.

Martin Zdravkov, 36, was frustrated by a Bulgarian court which, in early 2000, turned down his application to change his name to Manchester United.

The Chicago Theological Seminary has a Graham Taylor Chapel.

Michael Jackson also plays for Preston North End.

NATIONALITY

Irishman Elisha Scott, Scotsman Robert Ireland, Irishman Sam English and Welshman George Poland were all Liverpool players between the two world wars.

Celtic keeper of the thirties, J. Kennaway, won two caps for Scotland whilst playing there, but in 1928 had played for Canada against the USA, then in 1930 turned out for the USA against Canada!

Tommy Pearson of Newcastle played both for England against Scotland, and for Scotland against England. Pearson,

Football anoraks should know that Manchester United made ten thousand and **ninety-eight** passes in the opposition's half during Premiership season 1998–99 – according to Carling Opta statistics.

born in Edinburgh but with an English father, achieved the former in 1939 whilst standing in for a couple of missing England players. Then in 1947 he turned out for his country of birth against England.

Jack Reynolds won five caps for Ireland in 1890 and 1891 whilst playing there for Distillery. On signing for WBA it transpired he had been born in England – for whom he then won several caps.

NAZIS

When the Nazis took power in Germany in 1933 the chairman of Bayern Munich was Kurt Landauer, a Jew, who was sent to Dachau concentration camp before fleeing to Geneva.

In 1936, Adolf Hitler paid his only visit to a football match – storming out of the Post Stadium in Berlin after Germany went two down to Norway with five minutes left.

Prior to their 1938 international against Germany in Berlin, the English team controversially gave a Nazi salute before winning the match 6–3.

Striker Matthias Sindelar scored 27 goals in 44 internationals for Austria in the early 1930s but by 1938, with his country part of the Third Reich, he was forced as a Jew to wear the Star of David. Despite having qualified for the 1938 World Cup, the Austrians were absorbed into the German squad. Sindelar declared that he would not play in protest against the Nazi regime. In January 1939 he and his part-Jewish

The stand at Wolverton Town FC in Bucks, built in eighteen **ninety-nine**, is believed to be the oldest in the world.

girlfriend jointly committed suicide. Twenty thousand lined the streets of Vienna for his funeral.

Julian Hirsch and Gerhard Fuchs were the last two Jewish players to play for Germany. Hirsch was arrested in 1943 and sent to Auschwitz, never to be seen again; Fuchs escaped to Canada.

Aston Villa keeper Mark Bosnich was fined £1,000 after incensing Spurs fans with a Nazi salute at White Hart Lane in October 1996.

Hong Kong's most popular newspaper, *Apple Daily*, had to issue a public apology in April 1998 after illustrating a tribute to Germany's World Cup football team with a picture of Adolf Hitler wearing a swastika armband.

The Madrid regional government threatened legal action against Atletico Madrid in 1999 for failing to prevent their fans from displaying Nazi symbols at matches.

'If swastikas and anti-semitic banners continue to appear in Italian stadia, then the world of sport will decide to play behind closed doors.' Italian sports minister Giovanna Melandri who, in November 1999, warned that the country's football grounds were 'nurturing neo-Nazi extremism'.

NET

Port Vale striker Roddy Georgeson was given a mid-sixties debut by boss Stanley Matthews. So quick and enthusiastic

Of the 120,000 crowd who turned up in Tehran to see Iranian side Esteghlal beaten 2–1 by Japanese club Jubilo Iwata in 1993, just **one hundred** were Jubilo fans.

was the teenager that when he scored his first goal, against Rochdale, he had to be cut free from the net by the referee and officials after hurtling into it en route to the goal.

NO GOAL

Chelsea beat Ipswich 2–1 in September 1970 courtesy of a 'goal' scored by Alan Hudson, whose shot clearly hit the stanchion outside the goal and rebounded on to the pitch. Everyone prepared for a goal kick, except referee Roy Capey from Crewe, who signalled and awarded a goal. Chelsea boss Dave Sexton later commented: 'We all know it wasn't a goal, but he's given it, hasn't he?'

NO POINT

Possibly the most bizarre decision ever by a manager was Bryan Robson's refusal to go ahead with Middlesbrough's December 1997 Premiership game against Blackburn, claiming his squad was decimated by illnesses, injury and suspension. The FA docked Middlesbrough three points, they lost the rescheduled game and were relegated at the end of the season by one point. Robson kept his job.

NO SHOW

'One team in Tallinn,' sang Scottish supporters in October 1996 as their World Cup qualifying opponents Estonia failed to turn up at their own home venue for the game following a dispute over the kick-off time. Scotland took the field, the referee blew the whistle, they kicked off and the ref blew for full time. Scotland were awarded the match – but it was subsequently decided that it should be replayed. Estonia arrived at the appointed hour and held the Scots to a draw.

Huddersfield Town's most prolific year for League goals was in the 1979–80 Division Four season when they scored **one hundred and one**.

NUDE

Actress Sabrina Ferilli, 32, promised to strip in the centre circle of Roma's ground should they win the 1999–2000 Scudetto.

Reuters correspondent Eniwoke Ibagere was having trouble getting quotes from the losing African Champions Cup finalists *Zamalek*, who went down 1–0 to Shooting Stars of Nigeria in the 1999/2000 Final. So he stripped naked and strode into the changing room – whereupon the startled players agreed to talk to him.

NUMBERS

Brazil won the World Cup in 1970 and 1994. 1,970 + 1,994 = 3,964.
Argentina won in 1978 and 1986. 1,978 + 1,986 = 3,964.
Germany won in 1974 and 1990. 1,974 + 1,990 = 3,964.
England won in 1966. 1,966 + 1,998 = 3,964.
So why didn't England win in 1998?

Paul Gascoigne gave an insight in 1998 into his thoughts on the power of numbers: 'I have this thing about 4. I don't know why 4 – my favourite used to be 5 and then 7. Then I got into this thing about 13, where nothing would be done in 4s because 4 and 9 are 13. I don't know where 9 comes from. I got it into my head because 4 and 9 are 13. That's like 6 and 7. I can't bear to see them together because that's 13 again. So when I go out on to the park, I won't go out 6th or 7th. Nor 4th. It'll be either 5th or 8th.' Well, that's clear enough, Gazza, but aren't 5 and 8 13?

During the 1943–44 season, Notts County used **one hundred and two** different players.

OFFSIDE

Spectators all over the world muttered 'told you so' as scientific research in Madrid on the speed of focusing of the human eye, with particular reference to football's offside rule, was published in *The Lancet* medical journal in January 1998. It suggested that linesmen 'will inevitably have a false picture of players' relative positions at the moment the ball is passed'.

OPTIMISTS

Ever the optimists, Fulham, having lost 10–0 to Liverpool in the first leg of their 1986 League Cup tie, included in the programme for the second leg details of what would happen in the event of scores being equal on aggregate after 90 minutes' play.

OWN GOAL

Paul Flack scored a penalty against his own team in March

Paul Tait headed home after **one hundred and three** minutes of the Auto Windscreens Shield final in 1995 to win the game for Birmingham against Carlisle, Wembley's first Golden Goal.

1998. The 22-year-old skipper of Tap and Spile FC in the Scarborough Sunday League was outraged when the ref, Steve Ripley, awarded a penalty against his side, and whacked the ball past his own keeper. Ripley allowed the goal to stand, commenting, 'I thought if he was stupid enough to do it, I'd give the goal.' Tap and Spile lost 5–4 to Rangers Reserves.

When Bobby Williams, centre-half for Welsh side FC Maesteg, scored an own goal against Pencoed in January 1999, it was the 25th consecutive season in which he had netted against his own side.

Manchester City became the only club to score and also concede a century of First Division goals in the same season in 1957–58, with **one hundred and four** for and 100 against.

PANTS

Stoke striker Dean Crowe was ordered off during his side's Second Division game at Preston in August 1999 – for wearing the wrong colour underpants. Referee Kevin Lynch ruled that Crowe's blue pants, being worn under white shorts, clashed with Preston's blue shorts and sent the 20-year-old back into the changing rooms to swap undies.

PARLIAMENT

The Italian Parliament erupted into fisticuffs in April 1998 as it debated whether the referee should have awarded a penalty to Inter Milan after striker Ronaldo was fouled. Following the match, against Juventus, MPs questioned Deputy Prime Minister Walter Veltroni, alleging that referees consistently showed favour to Juve. Right-wing MP Domenico Gramazio became so irate that he had to be restrained by ushers as he tried to assault rival MP Massimo Mauro, a former Juve player, who taunted him with cries of 'Clown'.

PENALTY

ICIS League side Leighton Town were awarded two penalties within seconds of each other when they played Egham in September 1996. Ref Ian Trow pointed to the spot when Bradley Anderson was brought down. Anderson's kick was saved by keeper Trent Phillips and ran to Steve Norman, who was about to convert the rebound when he was fouled and a second penalty was given – which Anderson scored.

During an Arsenal v Liverpool game at Highbury on 24 March 1997, fans were treated to the bizarre sight of Liverpool striker Robbie Fowler pleading with referee Gerald Ashby not to award him a penalty following a collision with Gunners keeper David Seaman. Ashby insisted on awarding the penalty, although he didn't book Seaman. Fowler took a rather weak penalty which was parried by Seaman but put in by Jason McAteer, to give Liverpool a 2–1 win. Fowler's Liverpool team-mates had mixed opinions, but his action was widely praised – with FIFA secretary Sepp Blatter even going to the lengths of faxing a personal message to him.

Two days later Fowler was fined £900 by UEFA for exposing a T-shirt backing striking Liverpool dockers during a Cup-Winners' Cup tie, deemed to be a politically motivated action.

In a 1945 game for Kilmarnock against Partick Thistle, Tommy White took the same penalty seven times. The first six were ruled out as the referee ruled that the keeper had moved. The seventh was saved.

Forget Higuita and Chilavert, keeper Ted Scattergood of Derby and Bradford Park Avenue from 1907–25 scored eight goals – seven from the penalty spot.

Bobby Charlton scored a record 49 goals for England in **one hundred and six** games.

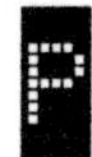

PERSISTENCE

After 85 defeats and one draw, Under-14s side Wootton, from the Isle of Wight, finally won a match in March 1999, when they beat Ventnor 3–2 to improve their goal difference of 64 for – and 959 against.

PHOTOGRAPHERS

Please avoid drawing stereotypical conclusions about the canny Scots from this information, but no photographic record exists of the first ever Scotland v England fixture, played in November 1872, because the 'photographic operator' entrusted with the job by the Scots refused to work without an assurance – which was not forthcoming from the Scottish FA – that players would purchase his pictures.

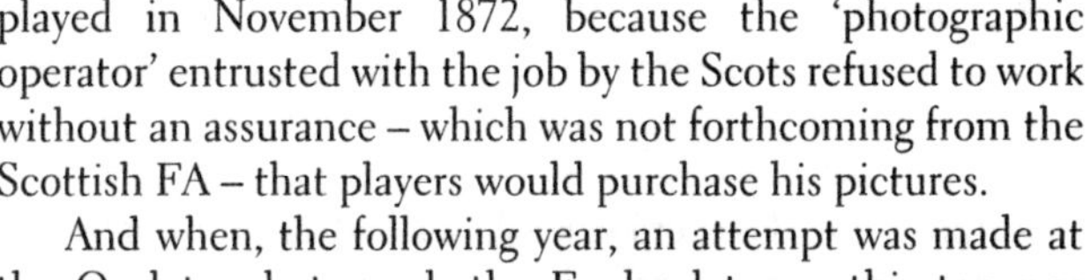

And when, the following year, an attempt was made at the Oval to photograph the England team, this too was unsuccessful 'because some of the team persisted in pulling faces at the camera'.

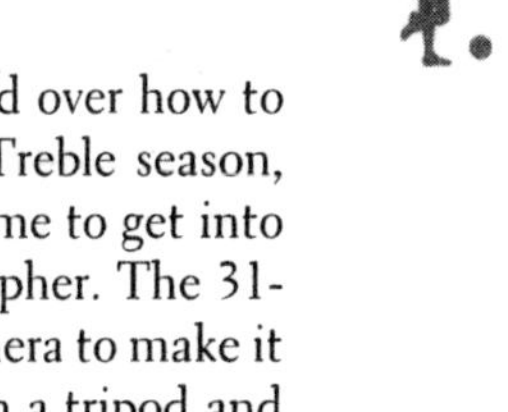

While other Manchester United fans agonised over how to get tickets for their biggest matches of the Treble season, 1998–99, bricklayer Mick Lynch hit on a scheme to get into games for free – he posed as a press photographer. The 31-year-old from Lewisham doctored a cheap camera to make it look more professional, equipped himself with a tripod and fold-up chair, invented a company name, UK Sports Media, and was soon finding himself sitting on the touchline with genuine snappers. He even made it into the Nou Camp for the European Cup final by making up a fake photographer's bib. 'A steward let me through the outside gates and I was on the pitch,' he told the *Daily Star*. 'I'd only just sat down behind Peter Schmeichel's goal when Bayern scored.'

Ian Dunn of Huddersfield became the first player in British football to win a game with a Golden Goal, when he scored after **one hundred and seven** minutes to beat Lincoln 3–2 on 30 November 1994 in the Auto Windscreens Shield.

PIANOS

Piano makers Yamaha revealed that football stars were spending up to £10,000 on grand pianos, in February 2000. Amongst those who had reportedly splashed out to tinkle the ivories were David Beckham, Sir Alex Ferguson, Gianfranco Zola, Sol Campbell, Ian Walker and Tony Adams.

PIGS

Sixteen severed pigs' heads were mounted on railings alongside six of Liverpool's main approach roads on 16 September 1999, apparently in protest at police handling of crowd trouble during a 3–2 home defeat by Manchester United.

Worthing United player Dave Clark faced an FA disciplinary fine after nailing a pig's head to the dugout of rivals Eastbourne in February 1997.

PLAY-OFFS

Play-offs are no recent phenomenon. In 1892 'test matches' were held in which the bottom three in Division One played the top three in Division Two in reverse order, to determine promotion and relegation.

POETS

Barnsley are one of the few clubs to boast a poet in residence – 52-year-old Ian McMillan. Another is Brighton's John Baine, better known to many as Attila the Stockbroker.

Alex Ferguson played **one hundred and eight** consecutive League matches for Swansea City in goal. No, not him – this was between 1928 and 1931.

POOLS

To the best of my knowledge pools companies don't claim a Royal Warrant, but it emerged in October 1993 that they might be able to boast of royal patronage. Author Andrew Morton, who caused a storm of controversy with *Diana: Her True Story*, revealed to the *Daily Star* that the Duke of Edinburgh was a keen, regular pools punter. The story included a comment from a 'royal insider' that 'the thought of Prince Philip checking his pools in front of the telly on a Saturday night will come as quite a shock to most people. They'll wonder if he puts a cross for no publicity.'

One wonders whether he picked his numbers by studying form, or chose numbers at random – how many diamonds in the old lady's tiara, or how many times the royal corgis messed on the floor that day.

Stuck for a way of picking his numbers, Sussex man David Rushen enlisted the assistance of his pet stick insect, which obliged by tipping enough draws to land him a £19.20 win in November 1993 after 49-year-old David lined its cage with 58 squares and let nature do the rest.

Eric Birks had a great system of using people's ages. The trouble was he couldn't remember how old his wife was. Forty-three, he thought, and put down that number, duly winning £138,000 – she was 42.

Forty-six-year-old bus fitter Mick Walters was dubbed 'The Most Honest Man In Britain' by the media when he split his £554,353 winnings with former boss Tom Neal. Some years earlier they had agreed to split their winnings should they ever hit the jackpot, and even though they had not seen each other for five years Mick honoured the agreement.

Hearts lost 3–1 to Hibs in a March 1882 Rosebery Charity Cup match, which raised **one hundred and nine** pounds for good causes.

Forty-seven-year-old Albert Horton received a cheque for £766.05 from Vernons in June 1992, which he immediately blew on a big night out for friends and relatives. Five days later Vernons were back in touch, explaining that they had sent the winnings to the wrong Albert Horton and had cancelled the cheque.

Four workmates formed a syndicate in 1990, apparently agreeing that they would make a joint entry. All winnings would be split, and should any of them win a million-pound jackpot via a solo entry they would give the other three £25,000 each. When Paul Pitt, one of the syndicate who all worked at a Portsmouth engineering company, won £1.8 million his memory of the agreement seemed to differ from that of his co-members.

The 28-year-old refused to hand over anything other than a round of drinks to Martin Foulds, Andrew Sullivan and Graham Ware. So the four ended up in court in September 1995 after the trio sued for breach of contract – and won. As well as the £25,000 payments, Mr Pitt had to shell out £14,000 in interest and up to £80,000 in legal fees.

In February 1980, brewery worker Dave Preston of Burton-on-Trent scooped the first dividend jackpot on both Littlewoods and Vernons in the same week, winning £953,874.10. Five years earlier he had won £10,000, and one week later he won again – 90p.

Pantelis 'Lucky' Menicou of Brighton failed to live up to his nickname in May 1990. Despite winning £216,000, he cost himself an extra £1.25 million by deciding to knock one selection off his coupon to reduce the entry cost.

James Brown, who played for both East Fife and Manchester United, left Old Trafford after **one hundred and ten** appearances in 1939.

In March 1984, three separate first dividend winners with Littlewoods were called Gamble, Luck and Riches.

Cameron Baxter, 27, was jailed for two and a half years in September 1995 when he pocketed the £5 stake he had collected from five Scottish Power workers instead of passing it on to Littlewoods. The five would have had the only winning line of the week and would have won £2.3 million.

Three friends who had filled in the same numbers on their coupons for 16 years missed out on a jackpot win of £600,000 when their collector failed to pick up their coupon because he was at a funeral. Bill Smith, Lenny Lowther and Frank Higgins were left fuming after their usual collector missed out on his round and arranged for someone else to collect the coupons in January 1994. His stand-in failed to show. The unlucky trio pleaded with Vernons to check their records to prove that they always used the same numbers, but they were out of luck – and vowed to switch to Littlewoods.

Sticking with the same set of numbers paid off in a big way in January 1994 for aircraft fitter Robert Slater of Bournemouth. On 1 January he won a fiver, missed out on 8 January, then on the 15th collected £15.75. On 22 January he won £16.35, but on 29 January his persistence really paid off when numbers 3, 11, 16, 18, 25, 29, 35, 37, 45 and 47 brought him £566,530.10.

A Brighton postman called Payne believed he'd discovered a first-class scheme to con his way to a massive pools win. The 26-year-old franked an envelope four days before the matches were due to be played and then filled in the results later on, sealing the envelope down and sending it off. He

Sunderland's Sandy McAllister went goalless for so long that fans promised him a piano if he netted. He finally did so on 5 January 1901 in his **one hundred and eleven**th first team game.

was exposed when his winnings were totalled up at £1.7 million and Littlewoods officials became suspicious. Payne admitted fraud and, in March 1991, was sentenced to 100 hours of community service.

Andy Paliunovas of Gloucester became the largest ever individual pools winner in January 1995 when he collected £2,326,792. The second largest is Dave Yeomans of Worcester, who won £2,293,110 from Littlewoods in August 1994.

A bizarre anomaly was thrown up on 17 January 1982 when, courtesy of the Pools Panel, Rangers were involved in two separate fixtures. They turned out on the park at Ibrox where they defeated Dundee United 2–0, but were also adjudged by the Panel to have been playing away at St Mirren at the same time where, perhaps even more peculiarly, they were deemed to have participated in a score draw.

Perhaps the most pointless outing of the Pools Panel came on 18 February 1989, when they sat in splendour at the Waldorf Astoria Hotel, London, to debate the result of a single game, the vital Beazer Homes League clash between Gosport and Ashford.

In 1964 author Roger Longrigg made a startling and perceptive observation which few before, or since, seem to have cottoned on to. In his book *The Artless Gambler* he drew attention to the fact that big pools winners have one thing in common: 'One quality, as many people have noticed, they share. They are all ugly. The explanation, if any, must be spiritual; it is fate's recompense for a great, fleshy nose, pig eyes, gap teeth, bad breath.'

Italian keeper Dino Zoff made a record **one hundred and twelve** international appearances for his country.

POSTMAN

One of the more unlikely career routes taken by a former footballer was that of Chelsea keeper Peter 'The Cat' Bonetti, who, after hanging up his gloves in the early eighties, opened a guest house and became post-master on the island of Mull.

PRISON

FC Brugge's Senegalese striker Khalilou Fadiga returned to his club from the 2000 African Nations Cup, only to discover that in his absence he had been sentenced to prison. He had taken part in an incident with supporters following a game three years earlier and in his absence had been tried and given a month's jail plus a £330 fine.

PROGRAMME

It could never happen today, but in 1915 Liverpool and Everton were producing a joint programme.

Sir Alf Ramsey managed England for **one hundred and thirteen** games.

RACING

Liverpool pair Robbie Fowler and Steve McManaman deliberately set out to confuse racing commentators by calling their first purchases Some Horse, and Another Horse.

RADIO

Broadcaster Danny Baker, a passionate Millwall fan, was sacked by the BBC from his controversial football phone-in programme on Radio 5 Live in March 1997 after abusing callers who rang in to support referee Mike Reed, who had awarded a controversial penalty to Chelsea with which they beat Leicester 1–0 in an FA Cup match. Baker commented: 'They can't allow a show like mine to be on the air and maintain their contacts at the FA.'

The move had been on the cards as Baker had previously said that the chairman of Millwall was 'bent', wished terminal illness on directors of Brighton & Hove Albion and 'urged death' on referees. Radio 5 Live controller Roger Mosey said: 'The problem was that he would not let anyone on the air disagree with him.'

A goal after **one hundred and fourteen** minutes for non-league Yeovil helped them pull off a great win when they beat First Division Sunderland in 1948–49's FA Cup, round four.

RED CARD

Referee Tariq Khan sent off striker Sean Nuttall during a Wakefield, Yorkshire Sunday League game in April 1999 – after he ran 150 yards to celebrate a 66th-minute equaliser for his side by diving into a duck pond. In his absence they lost 3–1.

Within 20 seconds of coming on, and before he'd touched the ball, AFC Chequers sub Dave Addison punched an opponent and was sent off in a Bedfordshire Sunday League game in January 1999.

Referee Terry Gilligan showed a red card to his linesman, Phil Cooper, during a tense Andover and District Sunday League game. Cooper signalled for a foul during the match between the Lardicake pub and Over Wallop Reserves in November 1998, but Gilligan overruled him. However, Cooper – landlord of the Lardicake – continued to wave his flag until Gilligan halted play and ordered the linesman off. Cooper refused to go, whereupon gas-fitter Gilligan picked up the ball and abandoned the match. The Hampshire FA fined Cooper £60 and banned him for 91 days.

There was little festive goodwill in evidence at Hull on 25 December 1936, when Wrexham's Arthur Brown was sent off within 20 seconds.

Billy Abercrombie of St Mirren was red-faced after a 1986 game against Motherwell, during which ref Louis Thow gave him his marching orders, red-carded him again for talking back and again for dissent. He was banned for 12 games.

Returning from a three-month ban for being sent off in the last game of the 1998–99 season, Port Vale's Tommy Widdrington lasted precisely one minute of his August 1999 comeback at Birmingham before being red-carded for a two-footed challenge.

Aberdeen striker Dean Windass received three sendings-off during a match against Dundee United. He was dismissed for two bookable offences, then his dissent earned him a further red card. He then ripped up a corner flag and threw it to the ground as he left the pitch, securing a further equivalent of a sending-off. He was suspended for six weeks after the incidents in November 1997 earned him a record 22 disciplinary penalty points.

Red-carded three times in a Scottish FA Cup game, for violent conduct, throwing his gloves at the ref and hurling his jersey in the same manner, Brora's keeper Donald MacMillan was handed a ten-match ban by the SFA in November 1999.

Having been shown the red card during a 1990 Italian amateur league game, Fernando D'Ercoli of Pianta snatched the card and ate it.

REFEREE!

By qualifying to become a referee, Sharon Duddridge was keeping it in the family in December 1998. For the 37-year-old from Newport was joining husband Steve, also 37, and sons Stephen, 14 and Stuart, 11, all of whom had already won refereeing qualifications.

It was not until the **one hundred and sixteen**th FA Cup final that a player was sent off – Kevin Moran of Manchester United in 1985.

A match between two Bristol Sunday League sides ended in chaos in November 1998 when two players were attacked by the referee. Thirty-one-year-old Kevin Jenkins officiated in the match between his own club, Sea Mills Park, and Backwell Sundays when the appointed official failed to turn up. However, Jenkins was already serving an eight-match ban – then, during the match, he punched a striker who called him 'whistle-happy' and head-butted another player who attempted to intervene. The game was abandoned and Backwell's secretary Jack Rebours commented, 'His refereeing was actually very good until he started hitting people.' Jenkins was banned for two years.

A ladies' soccer team in Scotland let the ref know exactly what they thought of him after losing a top-of-the-table clash 3–0, by using his kitbag as a toilet. The *Daily Record* reported in December 1997 that 'the foul play happened when Livingston Ladies were playing Monklands in a vital match' and quoted 'a source' as saying that 'the ref was absolutely revolted. I don't think he will be taking another one of Livingston's games.'

Referee Janet Fewings was sacked by the Devon County FA after the 42-year-old showered with the players in the Exeter Sunday League games she was officiating. Janet claimed she had joined the men to make a point about the lack of facilities for female referees, but was suspended for bringing the game into disrepute in October 1996. She was reinstated before finally getting the bullet, ostensibly 'because there were so many adverse remarks on her refereeing'.

Referee Jim Nitka was suspended for three months in 1997 after he slapped a player he had sent off during an Under-18s match in a Middlesex league.

Striker Trevor Ford played **one hundred and seventeen** League and Cup games for Sunderland from 1950–54, scoring 70 goals.

Hearts director Douglas Park was fined £1,000 in 1988 for locking referee David Symes into his changing room for 18 minutes after a game against Rangers.

After sending off an Oldham player who refused to go, referee H. Smith walked off himself during a 1914–15 game at Middlesbrough. Left-back Billy Cook was dismissed after conceding a penalty with a foul, then again fouling the same opponent. But despite being given a minute to leave the field he stood his ground – whereupon the ref departed, followed by both sets of players. The game was abandoned with Oldham 4–1 down. The result was subsequently allowed to stand but Cook was suspended for a year.

When he was jeered by sideline supporters, ref Keith Thompson responded by sending off the crowd. Fourteen supporters of Highbridge Town had travelled to Wyvern FC in Somerset for the local Saturday League game, in which Wyvern were leading 2–1 when trouble flared. Thompson had already red-carded two Highbridge players plus their manager Tony Turner when, with 20 minutes to play, he attempted to banish the 14 visiting fans – who included six children. He ordered them to the car park, before abandoning the match, after they questioned his decision to allow Wyvern's second goal following appeals for handball.

And ref Dave Warwick didn't mess about when an Under-11s game between Gillway Boys and Bedworth Boys at Tamworth, Staffs began to get out of hand – he sent the entire crowd off. 'Parents of both sides had squared up to each other and were shouting and swearing,' said Warwick in November 1995, so he warned the 50 spectators that unless they left he would abandon the game. They did and Gillway went on to win 4–3.

Arsenal nearly equalled their own record of 127 when winning the 1932–33 Division One title with **one hundred and eighteen** goals.

Psychiatrist Dr John Gayford booked all 22 players whilst officiating at a 1991 reserve team match between Croydon Municipal Officers and Merton Officers. 'Dr Gayford should get help,' said Croydon secretary Tony Osborn.

After being confronted at half-time over a decision he had made earlier during the Ryman League match between Farnborough and Purfleet in October 1999, ref Eddie Green decided enough was enough and promptly walked out of the ground, quitting refereeing there and then. 'I am no longer prepared to take the flak,' said Green later. 'It's the players who are the cheats now in my opinion.'

The referee red-carded the entire Crowmarch Under-13 side in October 1995 after their match, for singing rude songs about him.

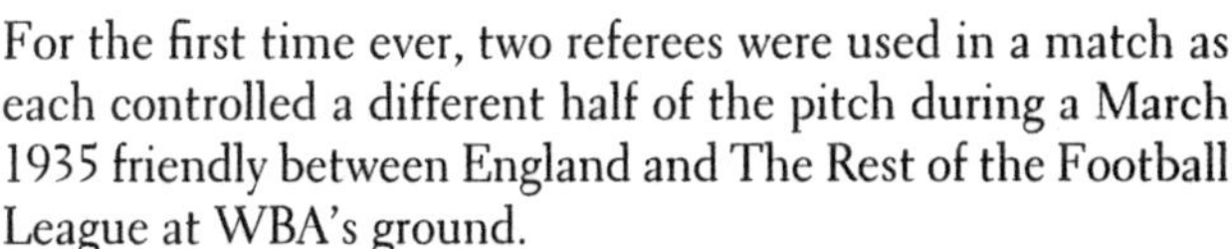

For the first time ever, two referees were used in a match as each controlled a different half of the pitch during a March 1935 friendly between England and The Rest of the Football League at WBA's ground.

Leading 16–0 with just half an hour remaining in an 1882 game, Birmingham City were slightly miffed when the ref abandoned their game against Darlaston All Saints.

An advertisement for Diadora UK which showed a football ref lying bound and gagged in the boot of a car was ruled 'distasteful' in September 1999, following complaints (but only four) to the Advertising Standards Authority.

Dog coat firm Barking Mad introduced World Cup kits for canines during the 1998 World Cup, which sold in Harrods for **one hundred and nineteen** pounds each.

'Referees should be wired up to a couple of electrodes and they should be allowed to make three mistakes before you run 50,000 volts through their genitals.' Aston Villa boss John Gregory in October 1999.

Assistant ref Wendy Toms was injured by the earpiece she was wearing to keep in contact with referee Rob Harris even before kick-off of the October 1999 match between Aston Villa and Liverpool. Wendy wrenched out the earpiece after hearing a piercing scream in her ear. Within 15 minutes she was white, shaking and in such distress that she needed medical treatment and missed the match.

Referee Ivan Robinson, albeit unintentionally, scored the winner for Barrow against Plymouth in 1968, deflecting a shot in from 15 yards for what proved to be the only goal of the game.

Gillingham chairman Paul Scally demanded a replay of his side's controversial 1999 Second Division play-off final against Manchester City after reports that referee Mark Halsey was seen celebrating after the game with City fans. The demand was refused.

REFUND

Two spectators got up, left their seats and demanded a refund 20 minutes before Huddersfield kicked off in their November 1998 home match against Bradford City. They had arrived 24 hours early for what they thought was an England rugby match against Italy.

Steve Cammack scored **one hundred and twenty** League and Cup goals during two spells with Scunthorpe 1979–86 to become their all-time leading striker.

REINCARNATION

Following his dismissal from the job of England coach, Glenn Hoddle may have been comforted to know that he was still being talked of as an international boss. For the news editor of an Indian magazine, *Maharaja*, wrote to his country's sports minister to propose that Hoddle be invited to coach the Indian squad for the 2000 Sydney Olympics. 'It would only be fit and proper that India, the land where the belief in karma and reincarnation originated, should offer Hoddle the job of training the Indian Olympic team,' said K.R. Padmanabhan.

RELIGION

Wolves made history by regularly fielding two clergymen in their side during the 1912–13 season – the Rev. Kenneth Hunt at half-back, and the Rev. Bill Jordan up front.

Hunt, in 1908, was also the last amateur player (and probably the last Reverend) to gain an FA Cup winner's medal.

After Ron Atkinson failed to keep Nottingham Forest in the Premiership at the end of the 1998–99 season, the club's local church put up a sign saying: 'So Big Ron can't save . . . guess who can!'

'God forgives even David Beckham,' read the sign outside the Rev. Andy Bruce's Baptist church in Nottingham following the England star's sending-off against Argentina in the 1998 World Cup.

Contacted by Fulham fan Ken Myers as they battled to win the Second Division championship in 1999, the Pope sent a

In their most prolific season Everton scored **one hundred and twenty-one** goals in the 1930–31 Division One campaign.

message saying that the club could be assured of his prayers. They duly won the title.

'We reported on April 9 (1999) that Pope John Paul II supported Fulham. We have been asked to point out that although the Vatican may have written to the club, the Pope is not a Fulham fan.' Apology to the Pontiff in the *Daily Star* of 24 May 1999.

Real Mallorca and Argentina goalkeeper Carlos Roa announced in June 1999 that he was quitting the game to dedicate his life to religious work. The 29-year-old, a member of the Church of the Seventh Day Adventists, was influenced in his decision by the fact that he and his fellow church members believed that the world would end in January 2000.

Plastic footballs featuring flags of the World Cup contenders had to be withdrawn from sale in Rotherham in March 1998 after complaints that the Saudi Arabian version featured a verse from the Koran. 'The Koran is treated with great respect,' said South Yorkshire local councillor Naz Ahmed. 'If you print a verse from it on a football and it gets kicked about in the mud it is a great insult to Muslims.'

A Swedish priest whose local side had lost four consecutive games – one 15–0 – called the players of Rumskulla GoIF into church for a special service during which they took communion, 'and then I passed the football from the altar down the aisle to the entrance of the church where the coach stood. It was symbolic. You have to pass to each other in life.'

Bo Stolpstedt was relieved when his prayers were answered and the side won their next match 7–0. 'Both my reputation and God's were on the line,' he commented in June 1997.

Middlesbrough hold the record for Second Division goals with **one hundred and twenty-two** in 42 games of the 1926–27 season.

Spanish side Villareal enlisted a little divine intervention to help them win promotion to the first division during 1997–98. Trappist monk Father Maria Vicente Ferrer played for the club in the 1950s before swapping his soccer kit for a habit. 'When they were in the promotion play-offs I rose at four in the morning and prayed all day in my cell,' said the 63-year-old.' I prayed to God and said that it would be my greatest happiness if Villareal were to go up. He answered my prayers.'

As any monk should know, though, happiness can be transitory, and during the next season Villareal were always struggling against relegation. 'This time I am praying for their salvation,' said Father Maria.

Wolves player Peter Knowles gave up the game in 1969 after he became a Jehovah's Witness, explaining: 'If you were on a football field and I had to stop you scoring a goal I would not hesitate to kick you. And that's not Christian.'

Irish bookmakers Paddy Power once offered odds of 10,000/1 that the Pope would sign for Glasgow Rangers – but later that season, the Pope broke his wrist. 'We offered to refund all stakes as we felt it would be difficult for him to take his trial at Ibrox,' said Power spokesman Stewart Kenny.

Cleric Don Finnermore tolled the bells of his church, St Peter & Paul at Aston, Birmingham, for three hours during the course of a Sunday morning Premiership match between Villa and Chelsea in March 1999. 'The game has disrupted the main weekly act of Christian worship at every church in the area. We are tolling the bell throughout the game for the death of the roots of the club, the values of the television company [Sky] and the faith of the fans,' said Rev. Keith Sinclair.

REPLAYS

Alvechurch and Oxford City were sick of the sight of each other after playing six FA Cup fourth qualifying round games in 1971. Alvechurch finally ended a sequence of results that ran 2–2, 1–1, 1–1, 0–0, 0–0 by winning 1–0 after an 11-hour marathon.

Tension mounted in the Devon League quarter-final penalty shoot-out between Morwenstow and Dolton during the 1998–99 season. After 22 kicks, Morwenstow were able to celebrate the narrowest of victories – at least until the league pointed out that the game should have gone to a replay.

With 15 minutes remaining at Highbury, Arsenal and Sheffield United were 1–1 in their 1999 FA Cup match. United kicked the ball out of play to permit treatment to injured Arsenal player Lee Morris. Ray Parlour took the throw, aiming to give possession back to Sheffield keeper Alan Kelly, only for Gunners striker Kanu to intercept the ball and cross it to Marc Overmars who put the ball in the net. Uproar broke out with Sheffield United boss Steve Bruce trying to call his players off in protest. Ref Peter Jones awarded the goal and Arsenal went on to 'win' 2–1.

Immediately after the game Arsenal manager Arsène Wenger offered to replay the match and within hours the FA had acceded to the request.

In 1887 Bolton won 1–0 at Everton in the FA Cup but the game was voided because they fielded an ineligible player. Everton won the replay but were then thrown out for using two banned players.

RING

Norwich fan John Jordan was shocked to discover a wedding ring in his shoe after he returned from a December 1999 game against QPR. He rang the club and discovered that it belonged to fellow fan Diane Thirkettle, who had lost it whilst applauding during the game and had given it up as lost.

RIOT

A riot broke out during the 1999 derby match between Athens sides AEK and Panathinaikos – unusually, though, it took place in the VIP section of the stands, where officials and the club presidents came to blows and had to be separated by police.

With his side three goals up against Palmeiras in the Paulista Championship finals in Brazil in July 1999, Corinthians' Edilson began juggling the ball. His showing off sparked a brawl amongst the players and a massive riot by fans. Edilson was later dropped from the international squad by coach Wanderley Luxembourg who said, 'I don't like his attitude.'

Spectators who felt they were being taken for a ride rioted and set fire to Hampden Park in 1909. At the end of the replay between Celtic and Rangers for the Scottish Cup, rumours swept around that the game would be replayed again rather than extra time being played, in order to boost gate money. The 60,000 fans were not best pleased so hundreds of them invaded the pitch after the players left, uprooted the goalposts, cut up the turf and set fire to various buildings.

Not everyone approved – the *Glasgow Evening Times* carried a letter suggesting: 'I would suggest the withdrawal of

Despite setting a record of **one hundred and twenty-five** goals conceded in the First Division season of 1930–31, Blackpool managed to avoid relegation.

all policemen from football matches and substitute a regiment of soldiers with fixed bayonets.'

ROYAL

When Prince Philip met Leeroy Thornhill of rock band Prodigy in February 2000 he asked whether the football club whose shirt the star was wearing were called Dreamcast.

In fact he was wearing an Arsenal shirt with their sponsor's name on it.

Jimmy McConnell notched **one hundred and twenty-six** League goals from 1928–32 to become Carlisle's all-time record scorer.

SACK

Jupp Heynckes coached Real Madrid to win the 1998 European Cup – only to be dismissed at the end of the season. In January 1991 the same club, then eight points clear at the top of their League table, had sacked then coach Raddy Antic.

A fan of a struggling Dutch first division side was so upset at their performance that he offered to foot the bill for the club to get rid of their inefficient manager. The anonymous supporter was frustrated when he discovered that FC Volendam could not afford to sack boss Dick de Boer, so he contacted the club and offered to meet the remainder of his contract from December 1998 until the summer of 2000 plus a substantial golden handshake, at a total cost of some 750,000 Dutch florins.

The club was appropriately grateful. Spokesman Cor Tol commented: 'If we had been able to sack him last season we would have avoided relegation.'

The FA Cup final managed quite nicely for **one hundred and twenty-seven** years before it was decided to introduce the penalty shoot-out to decide the outcome in the event of stalemate.

After losing 3–0 at Anfield under newly appointed boss Bill Lambton in 1959, Scunthorpe decided they had made a mistake and sacked the manager after just three days in the job.

Bristol Rovers sacked their tannoy announcer Keith Valle in 1991 after he announced, as rivals Bristol City brought on a sub, 'Here comes Junior Bent. I bet he is.'

After winning all six of their games, scoring 17 goals and conceding none in their European Championship Under-21 qualifying group, England sacked coach Peter Taylor in June 1999, for reasons not readily apparent to anyone other than the FA.

SEAGULL

When Danny Worthington launched a high cross into the box, it eluded all of his strikers – but hit a passing seagull on the beak and deflected into the net. Thirteen-year-old Stalybridge Celtic Colts player Danny was awarded a goal by ref Damian Whelan, despite one or two misgivings from opponents Hollingworth Juniors in the Tameside, Greater Manchester, Under 14 League. FA spokesman Steve Double commented after the September 1999 incident, 'To the best of my knowledge a seagull has never scored before. The referee was right.' The seagull, stunned after being hit by the ball, flew off, presumably to celebrate.

SEX

Promiscuous footballers are particularly prone to career-threatening arthritic knee injuries triggered by sexually

Aston Villa hold the record for First Division League goals, netting **one hundred and twenty-eight** in 42 games in 1930–31.

transmitted bacteria, claimed a report into research carried out by Dr Paul Oyudo. The findings of Dr Oyudo, studying for a Master of Science degree in sports medicine at Queen Mary and Westfield College in London, were revealed in *New Scientist* magazine in August 1999.

He investigated ten sportsmen, including five Premiership footballers, with persistent knee problems. At least eight appeared to be suffering from sexually acquired reactive arthritis, including all five footballers. 'The level of promiscuity among these sportsmen calls for concern,' said Dr Oyudo, recording that five of the sportsmen admitted having had more than 11 sexual partners.

Ute Winter, 29-year-old wife of a football club boss in Mainz, Germany was shown the red card by her husband after sleeping with 28 players – the entire first team, all of the reserves and many of the Veterans side, reported the *Fortean Times Book of Weird Sex* in 1995.

Research at Georgia State University during the 1994 World Cup final between Brazil and Italy revealed that levels of the male sex hormone testosterone in supporters of the winners, Brazil, rose by 27 per cent at the end of the game – and in Italian fans it fell by 26.7 per cent.

Hamilton Academicals player Gary Clark had to apologise in August 1999 after writing programme notes which described the team, featuring a number of young players, as being like a 'paedophile's buffet'.

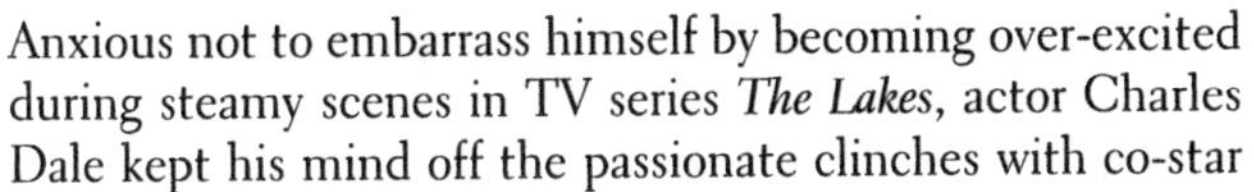

Anxious not to embarrass himself by becoming over-excited during steamy scenes in TV series *The Lakes*, actor Charles Dale kept his mind off the passionate clinches with co-star

Tony Kellow, with **one hundred and twenty-nine** goals in three spells between 1976 and 1987, became Exeter City's top scorer of League goals.

Clare Holman by reciting the England World Cup-winning team of 1966. He told her, 'If you hear me say "Geoff Hurst", don't worry.'

In 1967 Birmingham City came up with a novel idea for half-time entertainment – a 'leg-show' by local dolly birds, which went down well with fans. Officials, however, called it 'too sexy', after which the idea was dropped.

Beaten 15–0 by South Africa, the women of Swaziland's team claimed in January 1999: 'We lost heavily because all our coaches think of is begging us for sex. Anyone who refuses to sleep with the coaching staff is automatically dropped from the side.'

'I want to make love on cuttings from Manchester United's pitch,' gardener Kevin Handy from Luton told the *Sun* in November 1996, revealing that he and girlfriend Christine Murphy were turned on by the smell of grass: 'It reminds us of when we first made love on a freshly mown football pitch.'

Former Zimbabwe president Canaan Banana was jailed in January 1999 for allegedly having sex with an entire male football team.

Rochdale upset prudish fans when they launched their 1999–2000 kit catalogue, featuring topless models Jilena Hooton and Sarah Cooper. But the ploy worked, as merchandise manager Richard Wilde said: 'Sex sells. We have already beaten last year's record number of shirt sales.'

One hundred and thirty pounds bought an autographed photograph of Manchester United skipper and centre-half (1904–13) Charlie Roberts, at a 1989 auction.

Sex before a game may pep up the performance of footballers, was the well-received message from Italian scientists in November 1999. Emmanuele Jannini and colleagues at the University of L'Aquila studied 80 impotent men and discovered that a healthy sex life can boost levels of testosterone, the hormone related to sex drive and aggression. 'It's like starvation,' said Mr Jannini. 'When you don't eat you aren't hungry, but when you start to eat regularly then hunger returns.'

Conventional research had always suggested that abstinence benefited players because testosterone builds up if a player is deprived of sex.

'I make love a lot. It's the best recipe to be successful in football.' Chelsea star Roberto Di Matteo, March 1999.

'Good strikers can only score goals when they have had good sex on the night before a match.' Brazilian striker Romario, March 1999.

'I love tackling, love it. It's better than sex.' Paul Ince, 19 June 1999.

SHARES

Arsenal striker Davor Suker raised eyebrows in November 1999 when he bought £20,000 of shares – in Manchester United.

SHIRT

Pam Wilby was booked after scoring for Manchester United

Ladies during a televised FA Cup tie in October 1998 – after stripping off her shirt 'and waving it in the manager's face'.

Leon Jeanne of QPR was sent off in June 1999 after scoring for Wales Under-21s in their 6–2 defeat by Italy – for celebrating his goal by waving his shirt over his head.

It seemed disastrous for sponsors Holsten at the time. But it has now become a publicity coup for them that at the start of the 1987 FA Cup final against Coventry, dressing-room wrangling saw half of the Spurs squad appear with the sponsor's name on their shirts while the other half wore unmarked ones.

Newcastle fans draped the 65ft 'Angel of the North' statue alongside the A1 with a 29ft by 17ft replica Alan Shearer shirt in May 1998, after paying £1,000 to have it specially made.

'I wouldn't wash my car with that shirt now.' Spurs chairman Alan Sugar brandishing a shirt signed by Jürgen Klinsmann after he'd left the club. He changed his mind when the German later returned to play for Tottenham again.

When Roma's Francesco Totti scored against Lazio during the 1998–99 season, he whipped off his shirt to reveal a vest bearing the Italian equivalent of 'I've done you again'.

The cash-strapped Albanian FA refused to permit their players to swap shirts after playing Spain in September 1993, because they couldn't afford replacements.

Hearts scored **one hundred and thirty-two** goals in winning the 1957–58 Scottish League title.

Ref Dermot Gallagher sparked accusations of favouritism in January 1999 when, after officiating in a draw between Spurs and Wimbledon, he asked Tottenham's David Ginola for his shirt.

Birmingham midfielder Paul Tait was fined £500 after celebrating his side's Auto Windscreens Shield win over Carlisle in April 1995 by displaying a T-shirt with the inscription 'Birmingham City shit on the Villa'.

After scoring a late winner for Newcastle against Bolton, substitute Temuri Ketsbaia unleashed his frustration at being unable to hold down a regular place by demolishing an advertising hoarding, ripping off his shirt, elbowing a team-mate and taking his boots off before Magpies full-back John Beresford wrestled him to the ground.

'Almost every player went back to the hotel and made love to his wife with her wearing their husband's shirt.' Julie Jackson, wife of Everton's Matt, explaining how the side celebrated after beating Manchester United in the 1995 FA Cup final.

When Inter Milan played Manchester United in the European Cup quarter-final in 1999 their Zamorano wore the numbers 1 + 8 on his back – because Ronaldo was wearing the number 9 shirt he'd wanted.

Prince Rainier of Monaco purchased a Scotland shirt with the number 20 and name Rainier on it in 1980.

A female Spurs fan was spotted wearing one of the club's

away shirts with the word Arsenal printed on the back – underneath was the number 8, next to it the letters ER.

Inter Milan's highly paid players sported T-shirts calling for the dropping of Third World debts before kicking off their Serie A match against AC Milan in February 2000.

Chesterfield once wore shirts in a Union Jack design.

SHORT

Football's shortest player is believed to be the five-foot-tall F. le May, an outside-right for Thames, Watford and Clapton Orient in the early 1930s. He was dwarfed by 5ft 1in Crystal Palace winger C. Nastri, who played twice in 1958–59.

Shortest players to turn out for England were T. Magee of WBA, who won five caps in the 1920s, and Spurs forward F. Walden, who won two caps either side of the First World War. They were both 5ft 3in.

SHORT-LIVED

Depending on which source of statistics you believe, Jimmy Barrett of West Ham has the shortest England career on record, playing for between four and eight minutes against Northern Ireland in 1928 before going off injured, never to be selected again.

Peter Ward of Brighton's career also lasted eight minutes of a 1980 game against Australia, while Arsenal's Brian Marwood managed a minute longer against Saudi Arabia in 1988.

Suspicions were aroused in Yugoslavia when Ilinden FC won a match **one hundred and thirty-four**–1 in a 1979 match against Mladost, which assisted their bid for promotion.

SHOT

Despite being shot in the chest during a Unibond League game in August 1995, Winsford United centre-back Elfyn Edwards, 35, played on to skipper his team to a 1–0 win over Marine. Edwards said, 'I felt something hit my chest but I thought it was just a stone.' Then the linesman said that someone had fired shots at him and it became apparent that he had been hit by an air rifle pellet, fired by a spectator who escaped after being chased by spectators.

SIREN

Lincoln City fans sound an air raid siren when their side attack during matches at their Sincil Bank home.

SKULDUGGERY

1890 . . . Teams arriving at Shieldfield in Scotland to play local side Royal Oak would be warned that any goalkeeper foolish enough to prevent their star centre-forward from scoring, or saving his shots, was liable to have the utmost difficulty in departing from the ground with his limbs intact.

1900 . . . Jack Hillman, Burnley's goalkeeper, was suspended for a year after trying to bribe Nottingham Forest players to lose the game which would send Burnley down. Forest turned down the Burnley offer of £2 per head to 'take it easy' which, when they were 2–0 down at half-time, was increased to £4. No joy, though, Forest won 4–0.

1905 . . . Manchester City skipper and Welsh international Billy 'Prince of Dribblers' Meredith was banned for a season after trying to bribe Aston Villa captain Alec Leake for £10. Other City players were banned and manager Tony Maley was kicked out of the game.

Terry Venables was allegedly paid a one-off fee of **one hundred and thirty-five** thousand pounds just for entering into negotiations with club chairman Mark Goldberg, prior to joining Crystal Palace in 1998.

1908 . . . Leicester Fosse's England keeper A.P. Bailey was accused of taking bribes when he let in 12 goals during a game against Nottingham Forest. He was acquitted when he told the investigating committee that he had not fully recovered from a colleague's wedding two days previously.

1911 . . . Middlesbrough manager Andy Walker was banned for trying to fix the outcome of a game against bitter local rivals Sunderland which, indeed, Boro won 1–0. The game was allegedly fixed in order to assist Middlesbrough chairman Lt-Col. Gibson Poole's political aspirations. He was standing in the forthcoming General Election but, following the scandal, he was banned from football for life and lost the Election – none of which prevented him from receiving a knighthood on New Year's Day 1935.

1912 . . . Twenty-seven-year-old Richard McNeall was jailed for two months after admitting writing to Burnley and Norwich City purporting to be the goalkeeper of the teams they were scheduled to play, and offering to throw the games for £20.

1915 . . . After Manchester United beat Liverpool 2–0, having missed a penalty in the process, an investigation declared that the match was fixed. Although the rigging took place so that players could win money betting on the correct score, the result gave United the points which helped them avoid relegation, while Chelsea, who finished just one point behind them, went down. United's Enoch West was suspended for life along with seven others, and although the others so affected were eventually pardoned, his ban was finally lifted only when he was 62.

1919 . . . Most bribery cases are about those paying others to lose. East Dulwich bookmaker Henry Thatcher was given a three-month jail sentence, later commuted to a £50 fine, for trying to bribe two Millwall players – by offering them each £4 to WIN a game against Brentford, which they did. 'I did not realise I was doing anything seriously wrong,' said Thatcher.

At least **one hundred and thirty-six** Turkish MPs were reported to have been at the UEFA Cup final in Copenhagen in May 2000 as Galatasaray beat Arsenal to become the first side from that country to lift a European trophy.

1919 . . . Leeds City were expelled from the League for making illegal payments to players.

1924 . . . Sixty days hard labour was the sentence for former Scottish international John Browning and former Rangers player Archibald Kyle. Both had been found guilty of offering £30 to Bo'Ness players to rig their Scottish Second Division game against Lochgelly.

1941 . . . On Christmas morning, in the days before substitutes, Bristol City were playing at Southampton, but a number of their players were delayed and the game kicked off with City short of their full complement. At half-time, with City three down, their skipper Ernie Brinton arrived. He changed, rubbed mud over himself and slipped on to the pitch. Unfortunately for him he was rumbled by a linesman and sent off. Saints won 5–2.

1945 . . . On the ground that it could be construed as bribery, Grimsby Town were ordered to cease their practice of giving opposing teams a crate of locally caught fish.

1955 . . . Trinidadian player Selwyn Baptiste incurred the displeasure of the disciplinary authorities after being found to have played in a cup match the day after beginning a two-year suspension. They decided to increase his ban – by a further 998 years.

1969 . . . Accra Great Olympic FC of Ghana came up with a novel way of attempting to defeat their tour match opponents, Palmeiras of Brazil – Accra had 13 players on the pitch. An official later admitted: 'The two extra players sneaked on to the field, pretending to replace injured colleagues.'

1969 . . . El Salvador claimed skulduggery when they were beaten 3–0 by Haiti in a World Cup match after their opponents utilised the services of a witch doctor, who sprinkled strange powders on the pitch and chanted spells. The next time the two sides met, Salvador coach Gregorio

Bundi took appropriate action against the witch doctor – by punching him.

1970 . . . Off-the-field skulduggery was perpetrated against England's Bobby Moore when, a week before England began their defence of the World Cup, he was accused of the theft of a bracelet in Bogota, Colombia. Moore was detained by police as the squad flew to Mexico, but diplomatic intervention freed him and in 1972 a conspiracy case was brought against those who had made the original claims against Moore.

1971 . . . Officials of the Armenia Bielefeld team were found guilty of fixing four West German League games.

1973 . . . Following Leeds' 1–0 defeat by Salonika in the final of the European Cup Winners' Cup in Milan, Greek referee Christos Michas was suspended for cheating.

1977 . . . In an unprecedented scandal, England manager and former Leeds supremo Don Revie was charged by the FA with acting deceitfully and damaging the image of football. Revie had walked out on his country at a critical time, with a disappointing European Championship campaign behind him and an almost certainly unsuccessful World Cup qualifying schedule unfolding.

Revie, instead of watching opponents Italy, negotiated a deal to become head of soccer to the United Arab Emirates for a reported one-third of a million pounds before approaching the FA and asking them to pay up the remainder of his contract together with a £5,000 'golden handshake'. Revie, who revealed his plans in a *Daily Mail* article, was widely regarded as having perpetrated an act of treachery on his country and, in early 1978, the FA imposed a ten-year ban on him, although this was subsequently overturned in the High Court.

1978 . . . Scottish referee John Gordon and linesmen Rollo Kyle and David McCartney were suspended by the Scottish

Keeper Thomas Ravelli of Sweden chalked up **one hundred and thirty-eight** international appearances from 1981–97.

FA after revealing they had received presents worth £1,000 from Milan before a UEFA Cup match. Milan were fined £8,000.

1978 . . . Argentina needed to defeat Peru by a four-goal margin to reach the latter stages of the World Cup. Peru, who had been playing very well, collapsed inexplicably and were slaughtered 6–0. It was later alleged that Argentina shipped 35,000 tons of free grain – and possibly arms, too – to Peru while the Argentinian Central Bank coincidentally chose a similar time to unfreeze $50m in credits – for Peru.

1980 . . . Italy's top striker Paolo Rossi was amongst 30 players suspended as a result of an Italian match-fixing scandal. Milan and Lazio were forcibly relegated. Rossi was allowed back into the game in time to play and score vital goals for Italy's World Cup-winning side of 1982.

1986 . . . Roma were banned from UEFA competitions for a year after attempting to bribe the referee who handled their 1982 European Cup match against Dundee United.

1987 . . . Nico Ceaucescu, son of the infamous President of Romania, and President of Dynamo Bucharest, allegedly fixed matches so that his striker, Rodion Camataru, could score enough goals to win the European Golden Boot. It apparently worked – his tally of 44 was enough to land the award.

1988 . . . Hungarian international full-back Sandor Sallai and the country's former manager Kalman Meszoly were amongst 40 players and officials arrested in a match-fixing scandal. The next year, national coach Gyorgy Mezey resigned, complaining that he had no players left to pick.

1988 . . . Romania's ruling family, the Ceaucescus, controlled Steaua Bucharest before they were overthrown. In the Cup final in which they were playing, the referee had the temerity to rule out a potentially match-winning effort from their striker, Blint.

At this point the instruction went out to Steaua players

England's first manager Walter Winterbottom (1946–62) won 78 of his **one hundred and thirty-nine** games in charge.

to leave the field. The Minister of Sport then banned media from reporting the game before announcing the next day that the goal had been awarded and Steaua had therefore won the Cup. The referee and linesmen were suspended and all footage of the match destroyed.

1990 . . . On 28 May, the entire Albanian squad – all 37 of them: senior side, under-21s, coaches, doctors – were arrested at Heathrow Airport after over £5,000 of goods went missing from the duty-free shop. They were later released without charge, but a police official commented: 'It seems they did not quite understand the meaning of duty free.'

1990 . . . Chilean goalkeeper Roberto Rojas was banned for life after admitting cutting his own forehead with a surgical knife to feign injury during a World Cup qualifying game against Brazil in 1990, as a flare landed in his penalty area.

1990 . . . A disastrous year for Swindon Town. Following a hearing in February, their chairman, Brian Hiller, and former manager, Lou Macari, were found guilty by the FA of breaching their rule regarding betting on matches. Swindon, then in the Second Division, had visited Newcastle for an FA Cup tie in January 1988 and a £6,500 bet was placed on Newcastle, the 8/13 favourites, winning the match. They did so comfortably, 5–0, a £4,000 profit being made on the bet.

There were no suggestions that the match was fixed, but Macari was fined £1,000 and censured, while Hiller was suspended from the game for six months and the club was fined £7,500. Macari resigned a week later, although he has subsequently revealed that he intends to endeavour to clear his name even now.

Under new boss Ossie Ardiles, Swindon had won a place in Division One for the first time, only to lose their promotion and be forcibly relegated to Division Three for irregular payments to players. The punishment was later softened and they were reinstated to Division Two.

1991 . . . Jordanian side Al Ramtha withdrew from the

The Dutch squad for Euro 96 brought with them to England 900 pairs of shorts, 550 shirts, 500 pairs of socks and **one hundred and forty** jockstraps.

National League with three games remaining, claiming that the National Association was bribing referees to prevent them from winning the title.

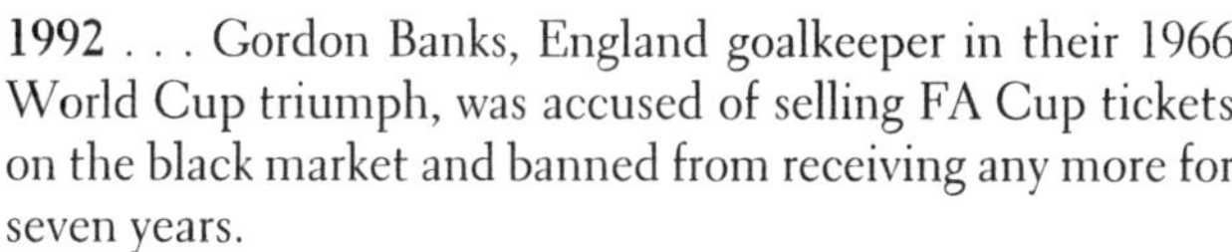

1992 . . . Gordon Banks, England goalkeeper in their 1966 World Cup triumph, was accused of selling FA Cup tickets on the black market and banned from receiving any more for seven years.

1993 . . . Irish side Linfield were given a bye into the first round proper of the European Cup after UEFA found their opponents, Dynamo Tbilisi, guilty of offering a $45,000 bribe to match officials.

1993 . . . Poland's League championship was awarded to the third-placed team after the top two, level on points going into their final matches, both won by unexpected six-goal margins. All four teams involved in the two games were fined £18,000 and both Legia Warsaw and LKS Lodz, the two title rivals, were penalised three points for the following season.

1994 . . . Spurs were fined £600,000, banned from the FA Cup for a year and docked 12 points from their next Premiership campaign after being found guilty by the FA of making irregular payments to players. However, the FA later backed down and reinstated them in the Cup, also handing back six of the points.

1995 . . . Fifty-eight players who had confessed to fixing matches in the Malaysian League were banned from playing anywhere in the world for between one and four years.

1995 . . . Politician and former president of Marseilles FC Bernard Tapie was sentenced to a year in jail for his involvement in match-fixing in the game between Marseilles and Valenciennes. Marseille player Jean-Jacques Eydelie, who handed over the 250,000 franc bribe to the Valenciennes players, received a year suspended and was fined 10,000 francs, while two Valenciennes players were sentenced to six months suspension.

Robert Cullingford was 16 years and **one hundred and forty-one** days old when he became Bradford City's youngest ever player in April 1970 against Mansfield.

1995 . . . Dynamo Kiev were expelled from the Champions' League and banned from all European competition for two years for allegedly attempting to bribe the referee of their home game with Panathinaikos. The Ukrainian club's general manager, Vasyl Babychuk, and director Igor Sourkis, were suspended for life from all UEFA-related activities.

1997 . . . Stevenage, champions of the Vauxhall Conference, were fined £25,000 (suspended for two years) and had to pay costs of £10,000 to the FA, for approaching Torquay in March of the previous year to offer them a deal designed to maintain their place in the Football League.

Torquay were bottom of the Third Division and facing relegation, but if Stevenage won the Conference, Torquay would be safe – Stevenage could not be promoted because their ground did not meet Football League standards. Stevenage suggested that if Torquay were to pay them £30,000 they would not sell their leading scorer, Barry Hayles. If they had done so, second-placed Woking, whose facilities were in order, might have overtaken Stevenage, thus potentially relegating Torquay.

1998 . . . Thailand and Indonesia were fined £24,000 each after being found guilty of both trying to lose a Tiger Cup match. The ASEAN Football Federation imposed the punishment after an Indonesian player deliberately scored an own goal, despite efforts by the Thai players to prevent him, in the final minute of the game in Ho Chi Minh City with the score 2–2. Neither side wanted to meet host country Vietnam in front of a hostile home crowd on Vietnam's National Day.

1999 . . . It was reported from Paraguay during September that two teams competing in a provincial league, both of whom needed hefty wins to boost their title hopes, won their respective matches 75–0 and 37–0. The league officials called an investigation into the 'possibility' of match-fixing when it emerged that the two losing teams had both started

Weighing in at **one hundred and forty-two** lb and standing 5ft 8in when he joined Norwich in 1914, inside-forward Charles William Christmas Abbs was born on 25 December, 1887.

their matches with just seven players. Cristobal Gamarra, 17, scored 35 goals in one of the games.

SMALLPOX

The semi-final of the 1898 Amateur Cup was played at a secret location in order to avoid the danger of spreading smallpox. Middlesbrough were playing Thornaby, but at the time there was a smallpox epidemic in lower Teesside, the area which was home to both clubs. The scheduled venue was Darlington, but residents there protested about the danger of the epidemic spreading if supporters arrived en masse, carrying it with them.

The FA then decided on an alternative venue which had to be kept secret, with the game being played behind closed doors in the hill village of Brotton in the Clevelands. Middlesbrough duly triumphed in front of a tiny turnout and went on to win the competition.

SMELL

Scientists seeking to discover which sporting activity produced the foulest smelling boots, shoes or trainers subjected hundreds of pairs to stringent chemical analysis. And football boots emerged at the very top of the pile, boasting a fungal count of 140,000, well ahead of second-placed ski boots with a rate of 100,000 and golf shoes with 93,000. The research was released in June 1999 after microbiologists at the British Analytical Control Agency completed their investigations.

SOCKS

Frank Leboeuf revealed in December 1999 that he and his French team-mates had real socks appeal – courtesy of the

national physio, who supplied them with newly designed socks to wear off the pitch. 'You have to have a hospital scan and blood pressure measurements on your calves. Containing nothing more complicated than cloth material they are then individually fitted to a specific pressure to help with blood circulation around the legs. They are a pain to put on because they are so tight and they have to be changed every three months. The main advantage of them has been in avoiding fatigue before and after games and on long trips.'

SOMERSAULT

Patsy Gallagher scored one of the game's most unusual goals in the 1925 Scottish Cup final when he equalised for Celtic against Dundee by somersaulting over the line with the ball wedged between both feet.

SPACE

When they signed Stefan Schwarz in summer 1999, Sunderland insisted that the player cancel the £95,000 ticket he had booked on the first passenger flight into space.

SPECS

West Ham full-back H.S. Bourne, who played for them from 1908–11, was one of the few bespectacled players to make it at the top level, as did Liverpool and Scotland centre-half A. Raisbeck around the same time.

Preston keeper James Mitchell played in the 1922 FA Cup final wearing glasses – and was beaten from the penalty spot by Huddersfield's Tom Hamilton for the only goal of the

Noel Cantwell, who played **one hundred and forty-four** times for Manchester United in the early sixties, also represented the Republic of Ireland at cricket.

game. In 1924 Mitchell won his only international cap for England, when he turned out at Goodison Park.

Despite having his glasses smashed early in the game, Feyenoord's Van Daele made a spectacle of opponents Estudiantes in the 1970 World Club Cup final by scoring the winner in Rotterdam.

Burslem Port Vale lost 10–0 at home to Sheffield United in 1892 but blamed the fact that their keeper lost his glasses in the muddy goalmouth.

SPORTING

With two minutes remaining and his side a goal down, coach Otar Korgalidze of Georgian side Dynamo Tbilisi might reasonably have been expected to be happy about a decision to award his side a penalty when a Lokomotiv player committed a dubious-looking offence. However, the sporting boss shouted at penalty-taker Ashvetia: 'Don't score! We don't need to win with a referee's help.'

The player ignored him and duly scored. Seconds later Tbilisi scored again to win the late 1999 game 2–1.

SPY

Exiled spy David Shayler, wanted by MI5 for allegations that he had revealed secrets about his profession in a book, managed to slip into England from his bolt hole in France to watch his favourite team Middlesbrough play Coventry in early 2000 – disguising himself en route with face paint in the club's colours.

Football League chairman Peter Middleton, who took the post in 1998, spent 16 years working as a spy for the Secret Intelligence Service, MI6.

SUPERSTITIONS

Superstitious Gillingham chairman Paul Scally blamed himself for his side's defeat in the 1999 Division Two play-off final, in which they had been two goals up with a minute to play. 'I remembered that the players were going to throw me in the bath if we won, so I took my wallet out of my pocket to protect it before the game was over,' he moaned.

Paul Ince would famously only put on his shirt after leaving the dressing room – or perhaps he was showing off.

England and Manchester United's Gary Neville doesn't sing the National Anthem before internationals as he thinks it might bring him bad luck.

Southampton fan Andy Richards eats woollen Saints scarves during matches, having first done so in 1996 when they beat Manchester United 6–3.

Terrorvision rock star Shutty, 31, owns a Leeds United scarf he has had for 25 years which he never washes and wears every time Leeds play.

Watford's Nigel Callaghan once revealed his pet superstition to *Shoot* magazine: 'I always eat crab on a Friday night.'

Newcastle's **one hundred and forty-six**-seat restaurant, The Magpie Room, became the first soccer stadium restaurant to appear in the Which? *Good Food Guide*, in November 1996.

Steve McManaman 'keeps a fake moustache in his car as a lucky charm', revealed *The Times* in February 1999.

'I always get my right leg ready first. And my right foot's always the first out of the dressing room.' Neil 'Razor' Ruddock of West Ham on his pet superstition. Ruddock also insisted on following the player wearing number 10 out of the dressing room.

During season 1938–39, in which Portsmouth won the FA Cup, the team underwent a bizarre ritual which involved outside-right Freddie Worrall buckling a pair of white spats on to the feet of manager Jack Tinn – left foot first – before each match.

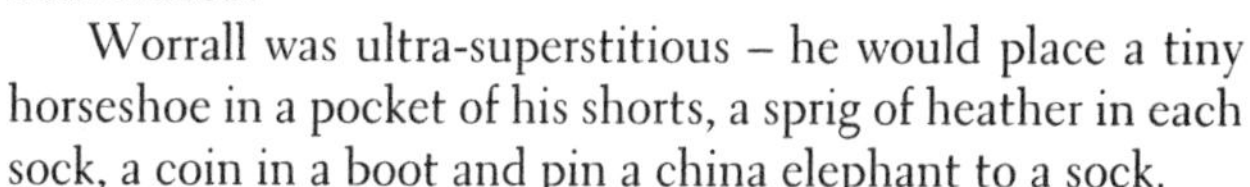

Worrall was ultra-superstitious – he would place a tiny horseshoe in a pocket of his shorts, a sprig of heather in each sock, a coin in a boot and pin a china elephant to a sock.

SUPPORTERS

When Blackburn Rovers came to the capital for the 1884 FA Cup final, the *Pall Mall Gazette* was not entirely sure about the club's supporters: 'London witnessed an incursion of Northern barbarians – hot-blooded Lancastrians, sharp of tongue, rough and ready, of uncouth garb and speech. A tribe of Soudanese Arabs let loose in the stand would not excite more amusement and curiosity.'

SWEARING

Stuart Pearce was announced as the 1991 winner of the PFA Fair Play Award in August but was then sent off for swearing whilst playing against Spurs on the same day.

FIFA credit Majid Abdullah of Saudi Arabia with a record total of **one hundred and forty-seven** international appearances, from 1978–94.

Refereeing Langley Park against Northallerton in a 1989–90 Northern League Second Division fixture, Colin Revel sent off both goalkeepers, each for swearing at their own players.

Kilmarnock's all-time leading scorer with **one hundred and forty-eight** goals is W. Culley (1912–23).

TATTOO TOO MUCH

Leeds United defender Michael Duberry boasts a tattoo across his shoulder blades reading 'Exodus 18:11' – a reference to the biblical verse: 'Now I know that the Lord is greater than all gods: for in the thing wherein they dealt proudly he was above them.'

Arsenal fan Jess Parnell has Manchester United's team crest tattooed on his backside after losing a bet. Forty-one-year-old Jess of Swanwick, Hants, lost the wager with 38-year-old friend and United supporter Paul Ridler. The pair had agreed that if either of their sides won the 1998–99 Premiership title the other would have that side's crest tattooed on their rear end. The only consolation for Jess was that the tattoo cost Paul £70.

Liverpool fan Dale McIntosh from Chatham, Kent, had Michael Owen's name and number, 10, tattooed on his back in August 1998.

Actor Sean Bean has '100 per cent Blade' tattooed on his shoulder. His actress wife Melanie Hill declared that football had ended their married life, complaining, 'We only had one night's honeymoon because of a [Sheffield] United game.'

Thirty-year-old Manchester United fan Shaun Southwick from Scunthorpe had all the club's League and Cup honours from 1892 to 1999 tattooed on his back.

Vinnie Jones . . . above left nipple.
John Hartson . . . Welsh emblem on right calf.
Stuart Pearce . . . right forearm.
Paolo di Canio . . . left upper arm.
Gianluca Vialli . . . large bird, right upper arm.
Lee Hughes . . . bulldog, left forearm.
Ian Wright . . . Harley Davidson, upper thigh.
Eric Cantona . . . Red Indian, above left nipple.
David Hopkin . . . right forearm.
David Beckham . . . baby Brooklyn's name on his back.
Marcus Bent . . . the Sheffield United player has two – a band round his wrist and a sun.

TELEPATHY

Uri Geller claimed credit for telepathically moving the ball on the penalty spot just as Scotland's Gary McAllister ran up to hit the penalty against England at Wembley in Euro 96 which was saved by David Seaman. The goalkeeper, said Geller, had been willed to dive to his right by the controversial spoon-bender.

By the time Scotland and England clashed again in their November 1999 Euro 2000 play-off first leg, the fickle Geller had switched sides, telling Scottish papers: 'I will be hovering over [Hampden] in a helicopter to amass the mind power of

Everton fan Tony Gawne paid **one hundred and fifty** pounds for a full-length tattoo of Duncan Ferguson on his back – 48 hours before the Scot quit the club for Newcastle in late 1998.

the Scots and make their team play better.' They lost 2–0.

TESTICLES

John Toshack was not sure whether the fans chanting his name when he took control of Turkish side Besiktas were being complimentary, after he was told that his name means 'testicles' in Turkish.

THROW

As of December 1999 Tranmere's Dave Challinor claimed the world record for length of throw-in, with a best of 46.34 metres.

TICKETS

The *Manchester Evening News* reported in February 1998 that a Manchester City fan who had thrown away his season ticket in disgust at the team's disappointing performances, had it returned by post three days later, with the anonymous message: 'If I have to suffer this rubbish, so do you.'

When tickets for the 1999 Euro 2000 play-off matches between England and Scotland went on sale, Wembley officials refused to sell tickets for the second leg to anyone applying by phone who had a Scottish accent. The blinding holes in the logic of this decision were implicitly admitted by a spokesman for Wembley, who commented: 'If anyone calls the box office and has a broad Scottish accent, sounding as if they come from Glasgow, then we will not sell them a ticket. But not all Scottish accents are broad. In fact, we all know Scots who don't sound Scottish at all. In some cases, you

Manchester United stars David Beckham and Ryan Giggs both paid a reported **one hundred and fifty-one** thousand pounds for Ferrari 550 Maranello cars in December 1998.

don't have to have a Scottish accent to be Scottish.' Following this announcement, 18 complaints were received by the Commission for Racial Equality.

Scottish officials duly applied much the same rules when tickets for their leg went on sale, although their much-hyped computer system, to deal with the expected rush of callers wishing to buy tickets, crashed almost immediately, allowing them to sell just two tickets in the first two hours of business. Later, it transpired that council workers from the office where the tickets were put on sale had short-circuited the system simply by dialling in on internal phones. The council announced that they would confiscate tickets bought in such a way – whereupon the workers went to court to confirm their right to keep them.

TIE

Wimbledon's Egil Olsen, dubbed 'surely the worst-dressed manager in football' by *Daily Express* writer Charlie Sale, was banned from Wembley Stadium's banqueting hall prior to the 1999 Charity Shield because he had no tie. Dons owner Sam Hammam reportedly shelled out £50 to buy a tie from a Sky Sports security man. Egil didn't know how to tie it.

TIME

Time-wasting can be a controversial part of the game. In 1892 Aston Villa keeper Dunning found the perfect way of ensuring victory for his side as time ran out for Stoke, who were desperately seeking an equaliser and had been awarded a penalty. Dunning promptly picked up the ball and kicked it out of the ground. By the time it was retrieved, the ref had had to blow for time. The rules were subsequently changed to permit an extension of time to allow penalties to be taken.

Arthur Rowley's **one hundred and fifty-two** League goals from 1958–65 set an all-time record for Shrewsbury.

TOILET

The *Football Fans' Guide* carried out a survey to discover the best and worst football ground toilets for season 1997–98. Queen's Park Rangers won the accolade for the finest facilities, while the most loathsome lavatories were deemed to be at Mansfield Town's Quarry Lane End.

At an auction in 1994 to dispose of items from Huddersfield's old Leeds Road ground, a bid of £70 secured Lot 83 – the toilet seat used by former manager Bill Shankly.

Bury went down 2–0 at Reading in a Division Two game in October 1999 and ended up with nine players. Not because they had men dismissed but because boss Neil Warnock, having already used his permitted three subs, withdrew two more players – Darren Bullock and Steve Redmond. He later explained, 'Bullock was elbowed in the face so I told him to come off. The other lad, well, he wanted to go to the toilet.'

TONGUE

Manchester City's Andy Morrison was sent off after sticking his tongue into Fulham's Stan Collymore's mouth during a confrontation in a First Division game during August 1999. Referee Paul Rejer handed out a second yellow card to Morrison for ungentlemanly conduct following his bizarre tongue-lashing.

TOOTHPICK

Billy Meredith, who won 51 Welsh caps between 1895 and

Craig Madden's **one hundred and fifty-three** goals from 1977–86 made him Bury's all-time top marksman.

1920, always had a toothpick in the corner of his mouth whilst playing.

TORTOISE

Fulham fans sponsored a tortoise at London Zoo, named Horsfield, in honour of their striker Geoff Horsfield in August 1999. 'I would have preferred a cheetah or leopard,' said the striker.

TORTURE

Sharar Haydar Mohamad al Hadithi, an Iraq international, was 'hit repeatedly' on the soles of his feet, dragged on his bare back through a gravel pit, and made to jump into a tank of sewage so that his wounds would become infected. He and other international team-mates were tortured on the orders of Uday Hussein, the country's dictator, alleged al Hadithi in August 1999, for not winning matches. Uday's former private secretary, Abbas Janabi, confirmed the player's revelations to the *Sunday Times*, alleging that he had seen players forced to kick a concrete ball around after failing to qualify for the 1994 World Cup.

TRANSFER

Former Newcastle defender Glenn Roeder would have been most people's idea of the last player Lazio were ever likely to buy. But they snapped him up in the early nineties – purely so that their real star signing, Paul Gascoigne, would have a mate to keep him company. Roeder was only required to kick the odd ball about for the reserves, and keep his pal on the straight and narrow.

Jim Towers hit **one hundred and fifty-four** League goals between 1954 and 1961 for Brentford, and 163 altogether to become their all-time leading scorer.

Inside-forward Abe Rosenthal was clearly torn between clubs during a career which saw him transferred from Tranmere to Bradford City, to Oldham, back to Tranmere, to Bradford City again, to Tranmere for a third spell, and once more to Bradford City, where he ended his career in 1955.

The Bosman ruling has come in for plenty of criticism, but England legend and Preston North End hero, winger Tom Finney, may well have wished it had been in place back in 1952 when the average wage packet in English football was under a tenner.

In 1952, Italian millionaire Prince Roberto Lanza di Trabia, president of Palermo, put a proposal to Finney: if he would agree to play for Palermo for two seasons he would be paid a lump sum of £10,000 immediately; his wages would be £130 a month with bonuses of up to £100; he would be given a car, a villa on the Mediterranean and a free passage to Italy for himself, his wife and family. The prince would also compensate Preston or buy him outright for £30,000.

'With great correctness,' said a contemporary account, 'he made an official request to Preston for release and the club, naturally, turned it down flat.'

Not many players have been transferred to two clubs at once. Playing for Millonarios of Colombia in the early 1950s, Alfredo di Stefano was bought by Real Madrid, only to discover that Barcelona also claimed him, having done a deal with his previous club, River Plate of Argentina. In the end the dispute went to the Spanish courts, which ruled that the player should play one season for Madrid, then one for Barcelona, and so on. Ultimately, Barca sold out their share.

Sunderland scored **one hundred and fifty-five** goals in 47 games during the 1889–90 season.

TURNCOATS

David Mellor switched from being a Fulham fan to support Chelsea.

Melvyn Bragg used to be a Carlisle fan but decided that Arsenal would be a better bet.

Nick Berry was reported in April 1999 to have deserted his long-standing favourites West Ham in favour of non-league Yeovil Town, whilst filming his TV series *Harbour Lights* in Dorset.

Endeavouring to promote his claims to win the race for Mayor of London, lifelong Everton supporter Steven Norris bought a £540 season ticket for Fulham in 1999.

David Neilson, alias *Coronation Street*'s Roy Cropper, started out as a Manchester United fan – 'something to do with the Munich Air Crash' – but defected to Leicester City in 1959.

Actor Kenneth Branagh was claiming to be a Spurs fan in 1999, having previously pledged allegiance to his home town Linfield and, whilst filming in Scotland, to Rangers.

In 1994 Labour MP Kate Hoey professed her support for Manchester United in an interview with Arsenal's *Gunners Magazine*. Yet by 1999, the year she was appointed Sports Minister, she was professing allegiance to the Highbury side.

Derby County were the most shot shy Premiership team of season 1998–99, hitting just **one hundred and fifty-six** on-target strikes, compared with most accurate shooters Arsenal, with 247.

Taking time off from winning the war, General Eisenhower visited the 1944 War Cup final at Wembley. He watched Charlton beat Chelsea 3–1 before commenting: 'I started cheering for the Blues, but when I saw the Reds winning I had to go on cheering for the Reds.'

Gillingham chairman Paul Scally used to be a staunch Millwall fan, but in February 2000 insisted that his allegiance had definitely changed – 'It's like re-marrying,' he said.

TV

Wolves threatened the BBC with a court injunction in 1965, claiming that a new drama series, *United*, was a thinly disguised version of the club's own situation.

'If you gave Arsène Wenger 11 players and told him to pick his team, this would be it.' You see what Andy Gray was getting at on Sky TV whilst covering an Arsenal game.

Explaining that he 'used to be a professional footballer', Teddy Maybank, who played for Chelsea until 1977, appeared on Cilla Black's *Blind Date* TV programme, sadly neglecting to admit the fact that he was married at the time.

Until overtaken by Ian Wright, Cliff Bastin held Arsenal's all-time career record of **one hundred and fifty-seven** League goals.

UMBRELLA

Aston Villa winger Charlie Athersmith, who in 1896–97 won almost every honour available – the League title, FA Cup and three England caps – once played part of a match protected by an umbrella borrowed from a spectator.

UNCONSCIOUS

Portsmouth keeper Aaron Flahavan rolled the ball out to kick clear during a Worthington Cup match against Blackburn in September 1999, only to collapse unconscious for no apparent reason. He had done exactly the same thing during a First Division match against Swindon a year previously – on that occasion the game carried on around him and a goal was scored. The 23-year-old underwent tests but they shed no light on the incidents.

URINE

Scunthorpe manager Brian Laws revealed one of his darkest

One hundred and fifty-eight illegally imported packets of cigarettes were collected after games at Arsenal and West Ham in 1999.

secrets in November 1999, confessing that whilst walking out of the tunnel at Wembley to play for Nottingham Forest against Luton in the 1989 League Cup final, 'The noise just hit me and I wet myself with the excitement. Luckily I was wearing white shorts.'

Four players from Zimbabwean club Tongogara were banned for life for urinating on the pitch after a witch doctor told them it would ensure victory.

Sunderland and England wing-back Michael Gray was fined £200 in January 2000 for urinating in a Sunderland shop doorway following a Christmas party.

George Brown's **one hundred and fifty-nine** goals from 1921–29 made him Huddersfield's all-time top scorer.

VIOLENCE

Soccer violence reared its head during a 1581 match between Cambridge students and their opponents, reveals a contemporary report: 'There was a match made betwixt certain schollers of Cambridge and divers of Chesterton to play at the fote ball, the sayd schollers resorting thither peacable withowte any weapons, the sayd townsmen of Chesterton had layd divers staves secretly in the church-porch and, in playing, did pike quarrells against the schollers, and did bringe owte their staves wherewith they did so beat the schollers, that divers had their heads broken.'

One Thomas Elyot declared in 1531: 'Footeballe, wherein is nothinge but beastlie furie and extreme violence, whereof procedeth hurte and consequently rancour, and malice do remaine with them that be wounded.'

A record crowd of 35,000, **one hundred and sixty** watched Toulouse entertain Moscow Dynamo in October 1986 at the Wembley-like Le Stadium.

WAR

War intervened in English football in March 1999 during the NATO bombardment of Yugoslavia. Crystal Palace midfielder Sasa Curcic, a Serb, walked on to the Selhurst Park pitch prior to their First Division match against Bradford, waving a placard reading: 'Stop Nato Bombing'.

Amongst leading figures in the conflict was Serb paramilitary commander Zeljko Raznatovic, known as Arkan, who in 1997 took over a lowly, struggling club called Obilic which promptly rose to become First Division champions. There were allegations that they threatened and bribed their opposition, and intimidated rival sides via their 'supporters' who included 'a core of shaven-headed men in black who chant death threats at players and opposing fans'.

And ethnic cleansing in Kosovo may have been financed by the £1.2m fee paid to Obilic by French side Bordeaux for Yugoslav international Yvan Vukomanovic, alleged French public prosecutors in June 1999.

Partizan Belgrade, however, benefited from the conflict as they were awarded the 1998–99 Yugoslav championship after 11 weeks of NATO airstrikes curtailed the season.

Ernie Moss's three spells with Chesterfield – 1968–76, 1979–81 and 1984–86 – brought him a club record of **one hundred and sixty-one** League goals.

Hartlepool United's ground was bombed by a German Zeppelin in November 1916, shattering their main stand. The club pursued the German government with a claim for £2,500 in compensation after the war, but were unsuccessful – indeed, the ground suffered further damage from another bomb during the Second World War.

In the 1945 Wartime South Cup final between Chelsea and Millwall, a system of 'guest players' had been permitted – only for both teams to abuse it to the point where Chelsea fielded eight guests and Millwall four. Even more absurdly, Scot Willie Hurrell, who played for neither Chelsea nor Millwall, was named as 12th man – for both sides.

During a similar competition, Fulham produced a team programme featuring a player called S.O. Else who was, it transpired, Some One Else!

Spurs' White Hart Lane ground was commandeered by the Ministry of Munitions in 1915 and was turned into a gas mask factory, producing 11 million of them in the belly of the stands by 1918.

Echoes of *Dad's Army* at Birmingham in January 1942. The club's main stand was being used as an auxiliary fire station. One of the firemen endeavoured to extinguish a brazier by pouring on it what he thought was water but turned out to be kerosene. The stand was burnt down.

Whether it was intended to help deal with unruly Ipswich fans isn't clear, but the Home Guard manned two gun emplacements in the car park at Norwich during the Second World War.

Between 1925 and 1930 Sunderland's Dave Halliday hit **one hundred and sixty-two** goals in 175 League and FA Cup games.

Malcolm Allison, then of Charlton, was called up to the forces in 1945 and spent three months in Austria, where he turned out for Klagenfurt and Rapid Vienna under the name of Herbert Schmidt.

During the Second World War there were a number of touring football sides which would play matches to help keep up the morale of the forces. These sides featured well-known players who had been drafted into the military. The best known were the Wanderers: a side led by Denis Compton toured India and another did likewise in the Far East, led by Tommy Walker.

The sides were as busy as the Harlem Globetrotters on occasions – the Wanderers played 13 games in 23 days on a tour of Palestine, while Compton's team went unbeaten for 50 games and played 33 times in the tropical heat of India, Assam, Burma and Ceylon, where games were limited to 35 minutes each way.

Not everyone was in favour of permitting football to continue when the First World War broke out. Historian A.F. Pollard wrote in *The Times*: 'Every club that employs a professional football player is bribing a much-needed recruit from enlistment and every spectator who pays his gate money is contributing so much towards a German victory.'

Bertie Felstead, the last survivor of the Christmas Day football match between British and German soldiers during the First World War in 1915, recalled the occasion in 1999, aged 105. The Royal Welch Fusilier spoke of leaving his trench near Laventie in northern France to share a cigarette with German counterparts, agreeing an impromptu ceasefire: 'We went to meet them and someone suggested football. It wasn't a game as such – more of a free-for-all. There could

Germany – East and West combined – have scored **one hundred and sixty-three** goals in the final stages of World Cups.

have been 50 on each side. I remember scrambling around in the snow but nobody was keeping score.'

Despite the fact that the Russians had just attacked its country and burned its major town to the ground, Terek Grozny, a side from Chechnya, applied in early 2000 to join the Russian Football Federation's regionalised Second Division, only to be rejected.

WEATHER

A match between Corinthians and Leyton in December 1894 was halted due to fog – which was so thick that the Corinthians keeper did not discover the match had been abandoned until many minutes later.

'A heavy shower' delayed kick-off of the 1879 FA Cup final by 25 minutes – wimps!

A little snow wasn't going to prevent appropriately named Gillingham skipper Mark Weatherly from getting to the ground for the match against Wigan in January 1987 – so he walked the six miles, only to find the game had been postponed.

A match at QPR in January 1999 was held up for ten minutes before the second half could get under way because of hailstones.

Michael Owen became England's youngest-ever scorer aged 18 years and **one hundred and sixty-four** days against Morocco in May 1998.

WEDDINGS

Wimbledon goalkeeper Neil Sullivan denied himself a honeymoon in order to play for Scotland against the Faroe Islands in a Euro 2000 qualifier in June 1999 – while teammate Don Hutchinson, who had scored for Scotland against Germany in his last international outing, opted to go ahead with his own honeymoon and miss out on the match.

Australian keeper Mark Bosnich, who had signed for Manchester United the day before, was arrested during his stag night celebrations and almost missed his wedding on 4 June 1999.

Paul Dickov had mixed feelings as he scored in Manchester City's dramatic late comeback from two down to win the 1999 Division Two play-off game against Gillingham at Wembley Stadium – for the keeper he scored past, Vince Bartram, had been Dickov's best man.

Hibs fans Maureen Cassidy and Paul Kirkland were married on the Scottish club's pitch in August 1997.

Spurs chairman Alan Sugar rearranged one of the club's 1999–2000 fixtures so that he could attend his son's wedding. Spurs were due to play West Ham on Sunday, 5 December, but this clashed with Daniel Sugar's nuptials. So Dad did a bit of wheeling and dealing with the Premier League, Sky and a number of other clubs and duly managed to swap Spurs' Sunday date with a Liverpool-Sheffield Wednesday match scheduled for the next day, revealed Mihir Bose in the *Daily Telegraph*.

Luther Blissett scored **one hundred and sixty-five** League and Cup goals in his record-breaking total of 180 career goals for Watford from 1975–92.

Salisbury pub player Steve Edgar proposed to girlfriend Donna McKay during a match in February 2000 – she said yes – he went on to score a hat trick.

WEMBLEY

Players would always say that the thrill of playing a game at Wembley Stadium could have no financial value. But in February 2000, with the demolition of the Stadium believed to be a matter of months away, an offer was put out to the public – hire the Stadium for a 60-minute match officiated by an FA referee. Both teams will be kitted out in England strip. Half-time refreshments included. Two match balls provided. Cost of the package: £28,000.

Clubs which have never played at Wembley:
Chester
Exeter
Halifax
Hartlepool
Hull
Lincoln
Rochdale
Walsall
Wrexham

WHO?

Bury were delighted with their new signing David Adekola, a 25-year-old Nigerian striker with 16 caps, 38 goals in 60 games for French side Cannes and 20 for Belgian First Division outfit Charleroi. Adekola had chosen Bury in preference to an £800,000 move to Marseilles so that he could be near his English girlfriend. He scored eight goals in 16 games, subsequently

Andy Turner of Spurs became the Premiership's youngest scorer aged 17 years and **one hundred and sixty-six** days against Everton in September 1992.

being loaned to Exeter and then to a number of other sides before signing in 1998 for Ryman League side Billericay.

But in December 1998 the *Observer* awarded Adekola the title of 'The Finest Walter Mitty Figure in the History of Football' after revealing that Marseilles 'have never heard of him', Cannes 'have never heard of him' and Charleroi 'have never heard of him'. His claimed caps cannot be traced, nor can the World Under-21 championship medal with Nigeria which he claimed. When confronted with these claims, Adekola, born in 1968, told the *Observer* he was 27 and about to embark on a Master's degree at the University of Kent.

WILLIE

'Have you seen his dick? Big? It isn't big. It's magnificent. I've seen some whoppers in my time, but Dion's is something else.' Alex Ferguson on Dion Dublin, quoted by author Rick Gekoski in his book *Staying Up*.

WORLD CUP WEIRDNESS

King Carol of Romania picked his country's side for the 1930 World Cup in Uruguay.

Bolivian referee Ulysses Saucedo awarded five penalties during the 1930 World Cup match between Argentina and Mexico.

Wearing spectacles didn't stop Swiss striker Kielholz scoring against the Dutch during the 1934 finals.

During the 1938 finals, Cuban keeper Carvajales was dropped,

Alan Cork is Wimbledon's top scorer, with **one hundred and sixty-seven** goals to his credit.

but called a press conference in which he predicted: 'The Romanian game has no more secrets for us. We shall score twice, they will score only once.' He was right.

Despite being invited to the 1950 finals by FIFA, Scotland refused to go because they had finished second to England in the British championship.

5–3 down against Austria in 1954, Switzerland issued a press communiqué at half-time, declaring: 'All goals scored against Switzerland owing to the sun.'

The Uruguayan team antagonised all other guests at their World Cup hotel in 1954 by continually playing a record proclaiming their virtues.

Uruguayan players were relieved when Hohberg equalised for them in the 1954 semi-final against Hungary. They congratulated him so comprehensively and enthusiastically that they knocked him out cold.

Contemporary reports claim that after Yugoslavia beat Uruguay 3–1 in the 1962 World Cup finals, the defeated side showed their appreciation of the ability of their chief tormentor, Yugoslav inspiration Sekularac, by carrying him off the pitch on their shoulders.

It could have been him! Burnley player Jimmy Adamson was offered the position of England manager for the 1966 World Cup before Sir Alf Ramsey got the job – but turned it down.

Simon Garner – who later played for Ryman League team Wealdstone FC – holds Blackburn's record for most League goals, **one hundred and sixty-eight** from 1978–92.

Nursing Times reported that following Ireland's 1–0 1994 World Cup victory over Italy, four supporters arrived at Dublin's St James's Hospital 'with bits of their ears missing'.

The Maldives set an unwanted World Cup record when they lost 17–0 to Iran in a June 1997 qualifying game in Damascus.

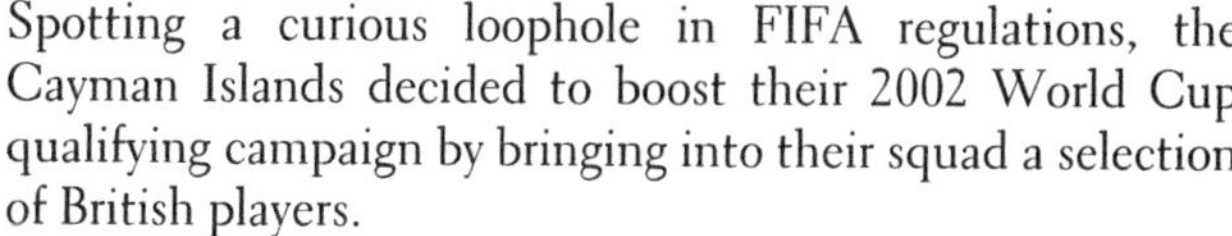

Spotting a curious loophole in FIFA regulations, the Cayman Islands decided to boost their 2002 World Cup qualifying campaign by bringing into their squad a selection of British players.

Bizarrely they selected, alongside the likes of Fulham's highly rated Barry Hayles and Tranmere's Wayne Allison, Ryman League players Dwayne Plummer of Chesham and Alec Masson of Bognor Regis – neither of whom could even make that League's representative side.

The move was frustrated two days before their opening game when FIFA banned the 'mercenaries'.

Sunday League players Damien Johnson of Kingston United and Andy Humphrey of Flackwell Heath pub side The Cherry Tree were slightly surprised to be called up for international debuts in a 2002 World Cup qualifying match for St Vincent against the US Virgin Islands. Johnson, who worked for the complaints department of a car hire company, commented: 'I didn't even know St Vincent had a team.'

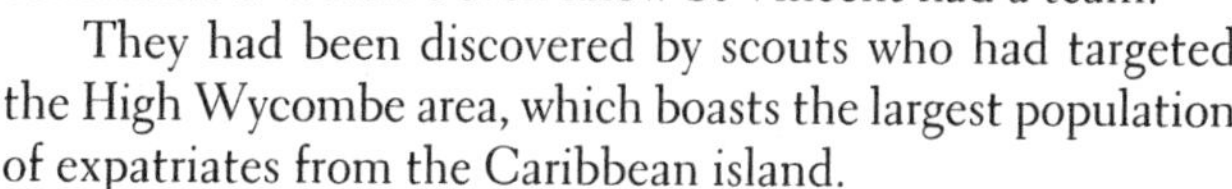

They had been discovered by scouts who had targeted the High Wycombe area, which boasts the largest population of expatriates from the Caribbean island.

Ken Burditt, who scored Norwich's first ever Second Division goal, made **one hundred and sixty-nine** League and Cup appearances for the Canaries from 1931–36.

YELLOW CARD

Paul Gascoigne was booked for booking the ref during a Rangers v Hibs game in December 1995. When referee Doug Smith's yellow card fell out of his pocket, Gazza picked it up and, handing it back, waved it humorously at the ref as if to book him. Showing a complete lack of humour Mr Smith promptly booked Gascoigne, who thus picked up a two-match suspension.

Vinnie Jones has twice been booked within five seconds of kick-off – playing for Sheffield United away to Manchester City in 1991, and for Chelsea against Sheffield United in 1992.

Florian Maurice of Marseille was booked during a 1999–2000 match – for taking his boot off and throwing it into the crowd after scoring against Paris St-Germain.

Hostage Taiwanese businessman Chi Chong Yi, whose Thai kidnappers were demanding a **one hundred and seventy**-thousand-pound ransom in July 1998, escaped when his guards fell asleep after watching the World Cup final.

ZERO

Swansea player Walter Boyd, who appeared in the Jamaican World Cup squad, acquired an unwanted record when he became possibly the first player ever to be sent off having spent zero seconds on the pitch. Boyd came off the subs' bench during a November 1999 home game against Darlington, became involved in some penalty area pushing and shoving – and was promptly shown the red card by ref Clive Wilkes. The official later confirmed that as the game had not been restarted, technically the sending-off had taken place when Boyd had been on the pitch for zero seconds.

Glyn Riley turned out for Barnsley against Torquay in January 1975 aged 16 years, **one hundred and seventy-one** days, to become their youngest ever player.

1 January 2000 . . . **FIRST** Premiership goal of the century scored by Branko Strupar for Derby after two minutes of their home game against Watford.

FIRST own goal of the century scored by Gareth Roberts after 38 minutes for Fulham at home to Tranmere in Division One.

FIRST penalty of the century awarded after 90 minutes for Reading, away to Gillingham, in a game which kicked off at 1 p.m.

FIRST yellow card shown to Darren Carr of Brighton after 12 minutes of their noon kick-off game in Division Three against Exeter.

FIRST red card of the century went to Bolton's Paul Ritchie for handball after 45 minutes of their First Division game away to Walsall.

FIRST Division One goal scored after 12 seconds by Bryan Hughes for Birmingham at home to Huddersfield.

FIRST still active 40-year-old player to receive MBE, Rochdale's Tony Ford.

FIRST Division Two goal scored by Nicky Southall after 20 minutes for Gillingham against Reading.

FIRST Division Three goal scored by Darren Freeman after two minutes of the Brighton v Exeter game. Freeman's goal was also **FIRST** of the millennium in British professional football.

2 January 1999 . . . Referee Paul Durkin asked for police protection during an Oldham v Chelsea FA Cup tie after being hit by a hot dog.

3 January 1987 . . . Liam O'Brien of Manchester United was sent off 85 seconds into their game at Southampton.

4 January 1999 . . . It was revealed that former Leeds and Sweden star Tomas Brolin had escaped unhurt after his car was in a collision with an elk.

5 January 1935 . . . After Arsenal's E. Hapgood took a penalty against Liverpool, their keeper Riley fisted the ball out only for Hapgood to head it back into the net.

6 January 1900 . . . After 65 minutes on a very wet pitch Stockport County were beating Haydock 5–1, and the referee refused Haydock pleas for an abandonment – so six of their players walked off. The game carried on and Stockport scored four more.

7 January 1899 . . . Rangers beat Clyde 3–0 to become the only side ever to go through a season with a 100 per cent record, having won all 18 of their matches.

8 January 2000 . . . 'I'm learning to control myself. I've got the message not to let myself get suspended again,' said

Chelsea's Gustavo Poyet scored a goal on average every **one hundred and seventy-three**.six minutes that he was on the pitch during the 1998–99 Premiership season, totalling 11 goals in all.

Tranmere's Clint Hill in the *Daily Star*, hours before he was sent off as they knocked Sunderland out of the FA Cup.

9 January 1954 . . . A record 15 third round FA Cup games were drawn.

10 January 2000 . . . Tabloid newspapers revealed that police foiled a £1m kidnap plot to snatch David Beckham's wife Victoria and baby Brooklyn, whilst he was playing for England against Scotland in Euro 2000 play-offs.

11 January 2000 . . . Aston Villa chairman Doug Ellis wore a red and white 'Santa hat' during his side's 3–1 win at Upton Park against West Ham in the Worthington Cup quarter-final.

12 January 1963 . . . 40 of the scheduled 44 Football League matches were postponed.

13 January 1990 . . . Preston, with 21-year-old Alan Kelly in goal, won 2–1 at Bury, who had his 23-year-old brother Gary in goal, in a Third Division game.

14 January 1933 . . . Arsenal, six points clear at the top of Division One, crashed out of the FA Cup 2–0 at Walsall of the Third Division North.

15 January 1972 . . . Swindon's record attendance of 32,000 was achieved against Arsenal in the FA Cup third round.

Tommy Lawton, aged 16 years, **one hundred and seventy-four** days, became Burnley's youngest player ever when turning out for them in March 1936.

16 January 1932 . . . F. Keetley of Lincoln City hit Third Division North opponents Halifax Town for six goals in 21 minutes.

17 January 1891 . . . Sheffield was the place to be for FA Cup goals, as Wednesday won 12–0 against Halliwell with Woodhouse netting five, while United crashed 9–1 to Notts County.

18 January 1998 . . . England were drawn with Poland in their qualifying group for Euro 2000 – the fifth consecutive time the two countries had been drawn together in major tournaments.

19 January 1999 . . . Russian former referee Nikolai Latyshev claimed that Tofik Bakhramov, the linesman who awarded England's controversial third goal in the 1966 World Cup final, was only selected to officiate after giving a referee's committee member two jars of caviar.

20 January 1923 . . . Celtic's Jimmy McGrory made his debut, going on to become the first player to average over a goal a game in British football – 410 in 408 games.

21 January 1961 . . . Would have been a blank day for football after Football League players threatened to strike if wage demands were not met. The tactic worked and the minimum wage was no more.

22 January 1927 . . . Listeners followed the action by means of a pitch diagram divided into numbered squares as BBC

Chris Hutchings was 36 years, **one hundred and seventy-five** days old in December 1993 when he became Rotherham's oldest ever player, in a League game against Bradford.

radio broadcast its first football match commentary – from Highbury where Arsenal drew 1–1 with Sheffield United.

23 January 1937 . . . Mansfield's Ted Harston scored seven times against Hartlepool in a Third Division North game.

24 January 1994 . . . England manager Graham Taylor was the subject of a Channel 4 documentary during the course of which he coined the phrase 'Do I not like that?'

25 January 1998 . . . Eric Cantona attacked a spectator at Crystal Palace where Manchester United were playing, with a kung-fu kick. He was banned for eight months, fined £10,000 and given 120 hours of community service.

26 January 1993 . . . Asked by Italian TV journalists for a comment, Paul Gascoigne belched into their microphones.

27 January 1996 . . . Southampton's FA Cup tie against Crewe was postponed due to a lack of toilet facilities.

28 January 1985 . . . Christine Walsh, wife of Republic of Ireland international Micky, gave birth to Liam, Kelly, Kate and Sarah – one of the very first examples of test tube quads.

29 January 1955 . . . Torquay's record crowd of 21,908 turned up to see Huddersfield in the FA Cup fourth round.

30 January 1937 . . . Of the 35 FA Cup and League matches

Essex side Dunmow FC ended the 1998–99 season with a record of nine goals for, **one hundred and seventy-six** against.

played on this day, not a single one produced an away win.

31 January 1953 . . . QPR defender Ingham scored against Gillingham from his own half of the pitch.

1 February 1936 . . . The 44 English League matches produced a record total of 209 goals for a single afternoon.

2 February 1929 . . . A late starter, obviously, A. Cunningham was 38 years, two days old when he took the field for his League debut for Newcastle against Leicester in Division One.

3 February 1999 . . . The *Independent* reported that 'Glenn Hoddle was sacked from his position as England coach last night after admitting a "serious error of judgement" in expressing controversial beliefs about reincarnation and the disabled.'

4 February 1998 . . . After Premiership Newcastle beat Conference side Stevenage 2–1 in an FA Cup replay, Newcastle boss Kenny Dalglish commented: 'We wish them well in the FA Trophy – we hope they get beat in the next round.'

5 February 1875 . . . Scottish side Queen's Park lost for the first time in their nine-year existence against Wanderers of London.

6 February 1997 . . . Former England striker Clive Allen made a significant career switch by joining the London

Eric Brook scored **one hundred and seventy-seven** goals from 1927–39 to become Manchester City's all-time leading scorer.

Monarchs American football side as kicker.

7 February 1931 . . . All five of Everton's forwards – Stein, Dunn, Dean, Critchley and Johnson – scored within 18 minutes against Charlton at The Valley in a Second Division game.

8 February 1902 . . . Kicking off for the second half of their FA Cup second round game against Lincoln, Derby's forwards and half-backs surrounded the man with the ball and guided the ball into the opposition goal area where Ben Warren whacked it in.

9 February 1878 . . . Hibs and Hearts drew 0–0 in the Edinburgh FA Cup final – and it took four more games before Hearts won 3–2.

10 February 1912 . . . An 'aggressive' pitch invasion led to the abandonment of Clyde's fixture against Rangers, who were held responsible and a 3–1 victory awarded to Clyde.

11 February 1939 . . . Birmingham's record crowd of 66,844 watched the game against Everton in the FA Cup fifth round.

12 February 1921 . . . Billy Meredith scored for Manchester United against Everton in Division One at the age of 48 years, 201 days.

13 February 1909 . . . Three times keeper W. Scott saved

George Best scored **one hundred and seventy-eight** goals for Manchester United.

penalties against Grimsby, only to end up on the losing side 2–0.

14 February 1998 . . . Substitute Brentford midfielder Scott Canham was voted Man of the Match in the Second Division game against Preston – despite remaining on the bench for the whole game.

15 February 1998 . . . US news channel CNN reported that Argentinian club Racing had organised a public exorcism of their stadium in an effort to improve their disappointing form. They lost their next match 2–0.

16 February 1993 . . . Keeper Scott Howie played in Scotland U21s' 3–0 win over Malta, kicking off at 1.30 p.m., and that evening in Clyde's 2–1 Division Two win over Queen of the South.

17 February 1973 . . . Kenny Hibbitt put Wolves a goal up at half-time in their home Division One game. In the second half Newcastle equalised, through Terry Hibbitt – Kenny's brother.

18 February 1982 . . . Bristol Rovers beat a team of prisoners 11–0 at Erlestoke Prison in Wiltshire.

19 February 1910 . . . Manchester United lost 4–3 to Liverpool in the first match at Old Trafford.

20 February 1998 . . . Distraught at referee Mike Riley's

failure to award Barnsley a penalty during their FA Cup tie at Old Trafford the Sunday previously, Barnsley's three Labour MPs tabled a House of Commons motion condemning the decision.

21 February 1998 . . . Butcher Len Howard started selling blue and white sausages, made with 'edible blue icing colour', to raise money for Brighton & Hove Albion.

22 February 1997 . . . For the first time, five players were sent off in the Football League when three from Plymouth and two from Chesterfield saw red in the last minute at Saltergate.

23 February 2000 . . . After England had drawn 0–0 with Argentina, 24-year-old Richard Buffrey from Ipswich was enjoying a drink in a pub near Wembley when a man asked whether anyone wanted to earn $100 for giving someone a lift to London. Buffrey found himself chauffeuring Argentina's striker Gabriel Batistuta and his family to his Sloane Street hotel.

24 February 1998 . . . While Watford chairman Elton John waited to be dubbed by the Queen to confirm his knighthood, he was introduced by Lord Camoys, the Lord Chamberlain, as Sir John Elton.

25 February 1967 . . . Having scored for Wolves at Fratton Park, Peter Knowles promptly kicked the ball clear out of the ground in celebration – only to be sent a bill for the cost of a new ball.

Luther Blissett is Watford's all-time leading scorer with **one hundred and eighty** goals.

26 February 1998 . . . Dundee United's Premier Reserve League match against Dunfermline, played at Arbroath, lasted just 90 seconds before being abandoned because of high winds.

27 February 1998 . . . 4–1 down against Burkina Faso in the African Nations Cup third-place play-off, Congo scored three goals in the last four minutes to take the game to extra time, and then won the penalty shoot-out 4–1.

28 February 1953 . . . Celtic's Charlie Tully twice scored direct from a corner – one effort being disallowed.

29 February 1992 . . . The final 60 seconds of the Third Division game between Birmingham and Stoke were played behind closed doors after the ground was cleared following a pitch invasion.

1 March 1980 . . . After watching his former side beat Liverpool 2–1, Everton great Dixie Dean died shortly after the match.

2 March 1998 . . . Lincolnshire non-league side Grantham Town announced that they were to replace former Prime Minister Margaret Thatcher as their president as she had 'not showed enough interest'.

3 March 1915 . . . The official attendance for Bradford City's 2–0 win over Norwich was nil.

Legendary early twentieth century star Billy Meredith played 670 times for Manchester City and United, scoring a total of **one hundred and eighty-one** goals.

4 March 1998 . . . Romanian player Ion Radu of Jiul Petrosani was sold to Valcea – for 1,100 lb of pork, worth about £1,750.

5 March 1959 . . . After playing a match, Birmingham City defender Jeff Hall became ill with what was revealed to be polio. He died two weeks later.

6 March 1875 . . . The Scottish Cup semi-final between Dunfermline and Renton was abandoned after 80 minutes when officials were unable to decide whether a shot from a Renton player had crossed the goal-line.

7 March 1965 . . . Real Madrid lost 1–0 at home to Atletico Madrid, having gone 122 games unbeaten on their own patch since losing 3–2 on 3 February 1957 – to Atletico Madrid.

8 March 1873 . . . A crowd of over 3,000 saw the first England v Scotland international to be played in England, at Kennington Oval Cricket Ground.

9 March 1974 . . . The sixth round FA Cup game between Newcastle and Nottingham Forest was declared void after a pitch invasion with the Magpies leading 4–3.

10 March 1998 . . . Perlat Musta, coach of leading Albanian side Partizan Tirana, announced that his side were to boycott the league because of assaults by fans on players and officials, only to be left in a coma after a neighbour shot him the next day.

Derek Fazackerley, aged 37 years, **one hundred and eighty-two** days, became Bury's oldest ever player in a League game in May 1989.

11 March 1962 . . . Burnley drew 4–4 against Chelsea, but played ten reserves as they had an FA Cup semi-final coming up. They were fined £1,000.

12 March 1982 . . . Ian Botham made his full debut for Scunthorpe, only to finish on the wrong end of a 7–2 thrashing.

13 March 1889 . . . The remaining ten minutes of a First Division game between Sheffield Wednesday and Aston Villa, abandoned through bad light the previous November with Wednesday 3–1 up, were played with Wednesday scoring again to make it 4–1.

14 March 1998 . . . Belgian special police announced that they had arrested seven Arabs following a siege in Brussels, smashing a plot to launch a biological weapons attack on the World Cup.

15 March 1920 . . . At the age of 45 years and 229 days, Billy Meredith turned out for Wales against England, becoming the oldest man to have played international football.

16 March 1985 . . . For the first time since 1912, Spurs won at Anfield, Garth Crooks scoring the goal which ended a hoodoo lasting 73 years to the day.

17 March 1991 . . . After testing positive for cocaine, Diego Maradona, who was playing for Napoli, was banned for 15 months.

Albert Quixall, who received £20 of his £45,000 fee from Sheffield Wednesday, played **one hundred and eighty-three** times for Manchester United, scoring 56 goals before leaving for Oldham in 1964.

18 March 1901 . . . Steve Bloomer scored four goals in England's 6–0 victory over Wales at Newcastle, becoming the first English player to score hat-tricks in different centuries – he'd done it in 1896 when England beat Wales 9–1.

19 March 1991 . . . After a world record 1,275 blank minutes, Atletico Madrid keeper Abel Resno at last conceded a goal, to Enrique of Sporting Gijon.

20 March 1966 . . . On display at the Central Hall, Westminster, the World Cup was stolen. It was later found by Pickles the dog, buried under a hedge.

21 March 1998 . . . The Northern Young Sinfonia Orchestra performed a live version of Prokofiev's 'Dance of the Knights' before Sunderland's First Division 2–1 win over Portsmouth. The music had been adopted as Sunderland's theme tune.

22 March 1949 . . . John Toshack, one of the few footballers to publish a book of poetry – *Gosh, It's Tosh* – was born.

23 March 1911 . . . Paris side Red Star's ground was inaugurated with a friendly between France and England.

24 March 1985 . . . Barry Venison of Sunderland became the youngest Wembley skipper as he captained his side to a 1–0 defeat against Norwich in the Milk Cup final.

25 March 1876 . . . Moses McNeil turned out for Scotland

Former FA supremo Graham Kelly walked the **one hundred and eighty-four** miles from his home in November 1999 to watch Middlesbrough play Wimbledon, to raise cash for charity.

against Wales, as did his brother, the less biblically named Harold.

26 March 1929 . . . Everton's E. Sagar joined the club – staying there as a player until retiring 24 years and one month later in May 1953.

27 March 1997 . . . Swiss referee Kurt Rothilsburger was banned for life by UEFA and FIFA for attempted bribery.

28 March 1985 . . . The North American Soccer League was discontinued.

29 March 1924 . . . Manchester City's Billy Meredith became the oldest player to compete in an FA Cup match as, aged 49 years and eight months, he was on the losing side in the 2–0 semi-final defeat by Newcastle.

30 March 1999 . . . A group of prostitutes threatened nude protests at the imminent World Youth Cup after being barred from hotels in Nigeria by tournament organisers.

31 March 1874 . . . Aston Villa's first ever match saw them take on a local rugby club, playing 15-a-side in the first half with an oval ball, 11-a-side with a round one in the second half.

1 April 1998 . . . Former Manchester United boss Wilf McGuinness turned up at Old Trafford for a televised disabled football supporters' tug-of-war contest that his

Mick Channon scored **one hundred and eighty-five** League goals for Southampton.

agent told him he'd been booked for by the 'AFD' company.

2 April 1992 . . . Cowdenbeath won 1–0 at home to Arbroath – the first time the 'Blue Brazil' had won in front of their own fans for 40 matches.

3 April 1915 . . . The referee sent Oldham's Billy Cook off with 35 minutes remaining of the First Division game at Middlesbrough. But with Oldham 4–1 down Cook refused to budge, and the game was abandoned.

4 April 1959 . . . Jeff Hall of Birmingham, who won 17 consecutive caps for England from 1955–57, died of polio aged 29.

5 April 1902 . . . Twenty-five people died and over 500 were injured when a stand at Ibrox collapsed during an international between Scotland and England – yet the game was restarted following a 20-minute delay, ending 1–1.

6 April 1994 . . . The FA called off England's friendly against Germany, which had been planned for 20 April – Hitler's birthday.

7 April 1900 . . . Playing in primrose and pink, the racing colours of Lord Rosebery, Scotland beat England 4–1 in Glasgow.

8 April 1944 . . . Just two hours after getting wed, Bradford striker Arthur Farrell turned out against Blackpool.

George Goddard, who played for QPR between 1926 and 1933, is their leading scorer with **one hundred and eighty-six** League and FA Cup goals to his credit.

9 April 1949 . . . Scotland beat England 3–1 at Wembley. The No. 6 button-up collar shirt worn by Manchester United wing-half Henry Cockburn of England in front of a 98,188 crowd, was sold at auction in 1998 for a modest £500.

10 April 1936 . . . Swansea won 2–1 at Plymouth Argyle in Division Two. The next day they lost 2–0 at Newcastle, having travelled a record 400 miles between matches on successive days.

11 April 1937 . . . When the French national side's opponents Italy pulled out of a friendly, Charlton stepped into the breach – and beat them 5–2 in the Paris game.

12 April 1924 . . . Everton's Sam Chedgzoy prompted a change in the game's rules when, playing away against Spurs, he took a corner, dribbled the ball past defenders and slotted it into the net. Nothing in the rules at that time prevented such a move and the goal stood.

13 April 1929 . . . Aberdeen's Alex Cheyne became the first player to score directly from a corner in an international when his 88th-minute strike at Hampden gave Scotland a 1–0 victory over England.

14 April 1945 . . . Contesting the second round of the Football League North War Cup, Cardiff and Bristol City played for a reported 3 hours 22 minutes in order to decide the game.

15 April 1923 . . . 85,000 saw Austria play Italy at Vienna's

Despite being a cult hero with fans at Upton Park, West Ham's Frenchman Samassi Abou played just **one hundred and eighty-seven** minutes for the club in 1998–99.

Hohe Warte and tragedy was narrowly avoided as wet weather caused sections of earth banking to subside.

16 April 1975 . . . Malcolm MacDonald scored five for England against Cyprus.

17 April 1897 . . . Aston Villa beat Blackburn 3–0 in their new Lower Ground stadium, which featured a cycle track staging professional racing – but a cyclist was fatally injured when falling on to the concrete track head first.

18 April 1989 . . . England keeper Peter Shilton's horse Between The Sticks won at Newmarket at 33/1 – but Shilton arrived too late to back it.

19 April 1985 . . . Chelsea announced that they would erect electrified fencing to deter hooligans, but the GLC threatened to take out an injunction to prevent the move unless Chelsea promised not to turn it on.

20 April 1974 . . . Bishops Stortford beat Ilford 4–1 to win the 71st and last Amateur Cup final.

21 April 1990 . . . Hereford player-manager Ian Bowyer, 39, and his son Gary, 18, both played in the Fourth Division game at Scunthorpe.

22 April 1989 . . . Every League match in the country kicked off at 3.06 p.m. – the time the previous week's Liverpool v Nottingham Forest FA Cup semi-final was abandoned as 94

Ken Foggo, who played **one hundred and eighty-eight** League and FA Cup games for Norwich between 1967 and 1972, played football and rugby union for England at schoolboy level.

people were crushed to death.

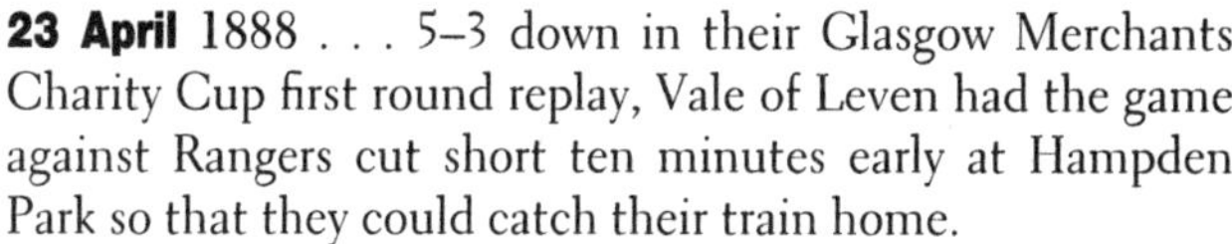

23 April 1888 . . . 5–3 down in their Glasgow Merchants Charity Cup first round replay, Vale of Leven had the game against Rangers cut short ten minutes early at Hampden Park so that they could catch their train home.

24 April 1915 . . . Bob Thompson of Chelsea was the first one-eyed FA Cup finalist. His side lost 3–0 to Sheffield United.

25 April 1914 . . . George V became the first monarch to attend the FA Cup final, seeing Burnley defeat Liverpool 1–0 in the last final played at Crystal Palace.

26 April 1919 . . . The cleanest international ever – only four fouls were recorded in the 2–2 draw between England and Scotland at Goodison Park.

27 April 1974 . . . Manchester United were relegated after losing 1–0 to Manchester City, whose goal was scored by Denis Law. Although the game was abandoned after an 82nd-minute pitch invasion, the result was allowed to stand.

28 April 1973 . . . Jack Charlton retired from the game – and on the same day, brother Bobby played his final game for Manchester United.

29 April 1967 . . . Coventry's record attendance was 51,455 for a Second Division game against Wolves.

Manchester United striker Tommy Taylor, a victim of the Munich air crash, scored 128 goals in **one hundred and eighty-nine** appearances for the club.

30 April 1927 . . . In the first recorded incident of a player dying during a match, Bury's Sam Wynne collapsed with a heart attack as they played a League match against Sheffield Wednesday.

1 May 1970 . . . A record 14,000 fans turned up to see Cambridge United's floodlights christened with a match against Chelsea – but with a crucial Southern League title decider the next day, the home side were replaced at half-time by Chelsea Reserves.

2 May 1980 . . . Keeper Bruce Grobbelaar scored a penalty for Crewe against York City.

3 May 1958 . . . During the FA Cup final between Bolton and Manchester United the red carpet leading on to the pitch caught fire.

4 May 1982 . . . A rare First Division 5–5 draw took place between Southampton and Coventry.

5 May 1951 . . . Stockport – featuring Alex Herd, 39, and son David, 17 – won 2–0 at Hartlepool in Division Three North.

6 May 1972 . . . Celtic equalled the previous record Scottish FA Cup final victory by beating Hibs 6–1.

7 May 1921 . . . A crowd of 13 turned up at Old Trafford to see Stockport – without a usable ground of their own – draw 0–0 against Leicester.

Trevor Senior scored **one hundred and ninety** goals for Reading from 1983–92 to become their top marksman ever.

8 May 1963 . . . With Scotland leading Austria 4–1 after 79 minutes of a game in which the Austrians had already had two players sent off, referee Jim Finney abandoned the game – a friendly!

9 May 1987 . . . Lincoln became the first Football League club to be automatically relegated to the Conference.

10 May 1977 . . . Austrian club SK Rapid opened their new stadium – designed by architect and former club striker Gerhard Hanappi.

11 May 1985 . . . The Third Division game between Bradford City and Lincoln, cut short by a tragic fire after 40 minutes with the score at 0–0, remains the shortest officially completed League match on record.

12 May 1971 . . . Gordon Banks had no saves at all to make, and touched the ball just four times from back passes, during England's 5–0 win over Malta.

13 May 1994 . . . BBC 2's inaugural *Fantasy Football* League title was won by presenter David Baddiel.

14 May 1966 . . . When they lost 3–2 to Everton in the FA Cup final, Sheffield Wednesday boasted a player making only his sixth senior appearance, Graham Pugh.

15 May 1910 . . . Milan's Arena Stadium staged the first ever Italian international match when they played France.

16 May 1987 . . . Coventry won the FA Cup for the first time, beating Spurs 3–2.

17 May 1997 . . . Roberto di Matteo took just 43 seconds to score the fastest ever FA Cup final goal as his Chelsea side defeated Middlesbrough 2–0.

18 May 1960 . . . Many people would vote for the European Cup final in which Real Madrid beat Eintracht 7–3 as the greatest game of all time.

19 May 1961 . . . Spurs beat Celtic 4–3 – in New York.

20 May 1980 . . . Manchester City's Joe Corrigan wore a bright yellow jersey as he played in goal for England in a 1–1 draw with Northern Ireland. It went for £520 at a 1998 auction.

21 May 1990 . . . Then playing for Newcastle, Mick Quinn had his first winner as an owner with Land Sun at Wolverhampton, trained by Mick Channon.

22 May 1977 . . . The *Sunday Express* revealed that Manchester United's Arthur Albiston, who had replaced injured Stewart Houston in a 2–1 FA Cup final win over Liverpool the day before, had offered his winner's medal to Houston – who refused it.

23 May 1926 . . . England beat Belgium 5–3, a game in which WBA's Joseph Henry Carter won one of his three caps – the one sold in 1997 at auction for £1,150.

Aged 16 years, **one hundred and ninety-two** days, Dave Buchanan turned out for Leicester in January 1979 to become their youngest ever player.

24 May 1964 . . . Manchester United's Noel Cantwell played for the Republic of Ireland in a 3–1 defeat by England in Dublin. His No. 3 shirt was sold at auction in 1998 for £420.

25 May 1911 . . . For some unknown reason Sheffield Wednesday were the visitors to play a Copenhagen team when Denmark opened their first fully enclosed football ground, the Idraetspark.

26 May 1909 . . . All-time Manchester United great Sir Matt Busby was born.

27 May 1998 . . . Michael Owen became England's youngest ever scorer in a full international in Morocco.

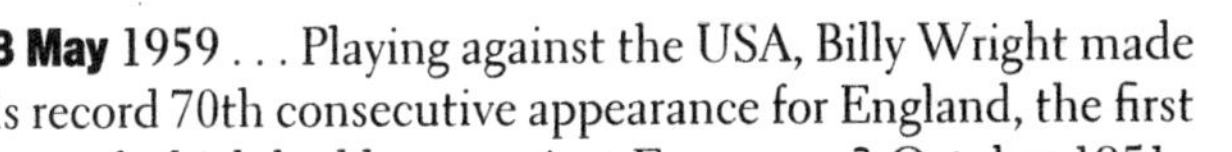

28 May 1959 . . . Playing against the USA, Billy Wright made his record 70th consecutive appearance for England, the first game of which had been against France on 3 October 1951.

29 May 1993 . . . Injured Paul Gascoigne wore a protective face mask in England's 1–1 draw in Poland.

30 May 1996 . . . Cathay Pacific claimed there had been £5,000 of damage to an aircraft bringing back England's players from Hong Kong amidst tales of a drunken binge.

31 May 1947 . . . Barrow's J. Kendall made an instant impact on his debut for the club, hitting a hat-trick against Rotherham.

Notts County's first ever floodlit fixture attracted a crowd of twenty thousand, **one hundred and ninety-three** to see them play Derby on 23 March 1953.

1 June 1953 . . . Arsenal and Scotland star Alex James died aged 51. His 1930 FA Cup winner's medal was sold in 1989 for £5,000, the highest figure achieved by one item in the inaugural Christie's auction of football memorabilia.

2 June 1891 . . . A meeting of football's International Football Association Board approved the introduction of the penalty kick.

3 June 1940 . . . Arsenal's Welsh international inside-left Leslie Jones played for Fulham. Two days later he turned out for West Ham, the day after for Southampton.

4 June 1963 . . . Norway beat Scotland 4–3 to land their first ever victory over one of the home nations.

5 June 1999 . . . Paul Scholes became the first Englishman ever sent off in a home international, receiving his marching orders during a 0–0 Euro 2000 draw with Sweden.

6 June 1908 . . . England played continental opposition for the first time, beating Austria 6–1.

7 June 1999 . . . Former topless model Samantha Fox kicked off the 'City World Cup' Human Table Football Tournament in Broadgate, London.

8 June 1999 . . . Five players were sent off during a friendly between Brazil, who won 3–1, and Holland. Three Dutch-

---

John Richards scored a record **one hundred and ninety-four** goals for Wolves between 1969 and 1982, later exceeded by Steve Bull.

men were dismissed.

9 June 1979 . . . Kevin Keegan's hit single 'Head Over Heels' was released.

10 June 1984 . . . England landed only their second victory over Brazil – the first had been 28 years earlier – when John Barnes and Mark Hateley both scored in a 2–0 win.

11 June 1997 . . . Mark Bosnich scored Australia's last goal from the penalty spot, as the keeper's country beat Solomon Islands 13–0 in a World Cup qualifier.

12 June 1938 . . . The first game played in Bordeaux's Parc de Lescure was a World Cup game between Brazil and Czechoslovakia, which featured three sendings-off and two broken limbs.

13 June 1986 . . . Jose Batista of Uruguay was sent off after 55 seconds of a World Cup game against Scotland.

14 June 1972 . . . One of the few stadiums in the world named after a bird, Belgium's Bosuil (Owl) Stadium staged the European Championship game between Belgium and West Germany.

15 June 1977 . . . Trevor Cherry became the third England player ever sent off – in a Buenos Aires friendly against Argentina.

During season 1998–99 the basic fee for a Nationwide League referee was **one hundred and ninety-five** pounds per match.

16 June 1982 . . . Bryan Robson scored the quickest ever World Cup goal, netting in 27 seconds as England beat France 3–1 in Bilbao.

17 June 1994 . . . Cardinal Basil Hume declined the opportunity to appear in BBC 2's *Fantasy Football* programme.

18 June 1992 . . . The *Sun* christened then England manager Graham Taylor 'Turnip'.

19 June 1965 . . . Hearts and Kilmarnock played an experimental match without offside. Hearts won 8–2.

20 June 1976 . . . For the first time a penalty shoot-out decided the outcome of a major tournament as Czechoslovakia beat Germany in the final of the European Nations Cup.

21 June 1920 . . . The date on the 15-carat gold presentation medal marking the appointment of William Struth as manager of Rangers (a position he held for 34 years) and sold in 1990 for £1,100.

22 June 1986 . . . No England fan – nor Peter Shilton – will ever forget the day when Diego Maradona put England out of the World Cup with his 'Hand of God' goal.

23 June 1984 . . . A record crowd of 54,848 filled Olympic Marseille's stadium to see France's European Championship semi-final against Portugal.

Keeper Chris Woods of Rangers set a British record in 1986–87 by going one thousand **one hundred and ninety-six** minutes without conceding a goal.

24 June 1990 . . . Holland's Frank Rijkaard received the red card for spitting at West Germany's Rudi Voller during a World Cup game.

25 June 1994 . . . Jack Charlton found himself with a £10,000 fine and touchline ban for allowing his Republic of Ireland players to drink water on the pitch during a World Cup match.

26 June 1954 . . . Austria beat Switzerland 7–5, a World Cup final stages record aggregate score for a single game.

27 June 1954 . . . Yugoslavia played West Germany in the World Cup quarter-final – the programme was sold at auction in 1998 for £650.

28 June 1999 . . . The FA announced that they were offering holders Manchester United the unprecedented option of pulling out of the FA Cup in order to concentrate on winning the World Club Championship. They accepted.

29 June 1999 . . . After being disbanded by the Serbs nine years previously, Kosovo's top Albanian side, Pristina FC, the 'Blue Boys', were again able to train at their stadium – which had first to be cleared of mines.

30 June 1940 . . . Some Roma fans still feel their team are homeless – this was the date they played their final game at the Campo Testaccio ground.

Pat Glover scored **one hundred and ninety-seven** times between 1930 and 1939 to become Grimsby Town's all-time top scorer.

1 July 1992 . . . AC Milan set a world transfer record by paying £13 million for Gianluigi Lentini from Torino.

2 July 1992 . . . The FA announced that referees in the Premier League would wear green.

3 July 1999 . . . All six races at Wolverhampton racetrack were named in honour of long-serving Wolves keeper Mike Stowell.

4 July 1999 . . . The worlds of football and pop music combined as Manchester United and England's David Beckham wed Spice Girl Victoria Adams in Dublin.

5 July 1999 . . . Argentinian striker Martin 'El Loco' Palmero was genuinely mad after he failed three times from the penalty spot in a Copa America match against Colombia.

6 July 1980 . . . Jim Corbett's birthday – he went from selling programmes at Gillingham, to playing for the first team, to joining Blackburn for £500,000 plus in the space of a year.

7 July 1999 . . . Speaking at his first press conference since taking over as manager of Wimbledon, Egil Olsen declared: 'I have always said I'd only leave Norway for Wimbledon or Brazil, but Brazil never offered me the job.'

8 July 1990 . . . Italy's Stadio Olimpico was renovated and ready for the World Cup final with just a day to spare.

One hundred and ninety-eight countries set out in pursuit of the 2002 World Cup.

9 July 1934 . . . Versatility should have been the middle name of Graham Shaw, born on this date. He played football for Doncaster and Sheffield United, was an English ABA boxing champion and played cricket for Yorkshire colts.

10 July 1978 . . . Spurs boss Keith Burkinshaw set a modern trend by signing Argentinian stars Ossie Ardiles and Ricky Villa for Spurs for £325,000.

11 July 2000 . . . Flying into Heathrow to join Arsenal, £6 million Brazilian Edu, was sent home for travelling on an illegal passport.

12 July 1953 . . . Hamburg's Volksparkstadion, originally built in 1925, was refurbished and reopened with a game between Hamburg and Birmingham. The stadium is not actually in Hamburg, but in Altona.

13 July 1930 . . . France's Lucien Laurent scored the first ever World Cup goal.

14 July 1999 . . . The *Daily Star* claimed that Manchester United manager Alex Ferguson might need a jaw operation as a result of chewing too much gum.

15 July 1999 . . . Arsenal were not best pleased as Spurs pulled off a cheeky advertising stunt by beaming images of their new kit via a laser projector on to the outside wall of Highbury Stadium.

Aberdeen's leading all-time scorer is Joe Harper with **one hundred and ninety-nine** goals to his credit.

16 July 1950 . . . A reported record crowd of 199,854 were in the Maracana Stadium for Brazil's home game with Uruguay.

17 July 1982 . . . Kevin Keegan was a guest on TV's *Little and Large* show.

18 July 1922 . . . Birth date of Liverpool loyalist Ray Lambert, who was with the club for 24 years having been signed on by them at the incredible age of 13.

19 July 1999 . . . Claire Holtby, 32, a mother of two from York, was given a six-month conditional discharge after becoming the first woman to run topless on to the pitch at Wembley Stadium, during the First Division play-off.

20 July 1871 . . . FA Secretary Charles Alcock put a proposal to the FA Committee to introduce a knockout competition – a Challenge Cup. Thus was born the FA Cup.

21 July 1951 . . . England beat Australia 5–0 to wrap up a tour during which they scored 32 goals against just two.

22 July 1928 . . . The most prominent chin in football – the one belonging to Jimmy Hill – came into being.

23 July 1994 . . . Maurice Remington of Leicester won the largest ever summer pools win, courtesy of Littlewoods – £2,281,399.

Godfrey Ingram became Cardiff's record signing in September 1982 when he was bought for **two hundred** thousand pounds from San Jose Earthquakes.

24 July 1966 . . . Birth date of Martin Keown, who in 1993 made Arsenal history by becoming the first player since the war to re-sign for the club, having been an apprentice there until 1986.

25 July 1986 . . . The roof of Real Valladolid Deportivo's stadium was blown off its frame by 80 km per hour winds.

26 July 1966 . . . 94,000 saw England beat Portugal 2–1 in the World Cup semi-final. The shirt worn that day by Portuguese winger Antonio Simoes raised £2,300 at auction in 1998.

27 July 1961 . . . The *Daily Mirror* revealed that Manchester United had signed former Manchester City player Alec Herd's son, David, for £38,000 – his dead-ball shot was later timed at 72.5 mph, beating all his team-mates.

28 July 1985 . . . Leeds hosted a match between the England and West German 1966 World Cup final sides in aid of the Bradford City fire victims. Geoff Hurst scored a hat-trick.

29 July 1977 . . . Chelsea's Eddie McCreadie quit the club, reportedly because they wouldn't give him a car.

30 July 1991 . . . The Hull City Handicap, run at Beverley in tribute to the football team, caused controversy when it was started one minute six seconds early and therefore voided.

Mick Channon notched a record **two hundred and one** League and FA Cup goals for Southampton during his career there between 1966 and 1982.

31 July 1999 . . . A paying crowd of 29 turned up to see Clydebank lose to East Stirling in the Scottish League Cup.

1 August 1974 . . . Brian Clough became manager of Leeds – for just 44 days.

2 August 1966 . . . Bulgarian hero Hristo Stoichkov was born.

3 August 1971 . . . Pickles the dog, famous for discovering the World Cup when it went missing, strangled himself on his lead whilst chasing a rabbit.

4 August 1938 . . . The £14,000 Arsenal paid Wolves for Bryn Jones was a British record for the next nine years.

5 August 1999 . . . Manchester United's Teddy Sheringham was thrown off a Cheshire golf course – for wearing white ankle socks.

6 August 1994 . . . Stoat stopped play at Watford where they were entertaining Spurs. Watford's Hornet mascot and Spurs keeper Ian Walker chased the animal from the pitch.

7 August 1999 . . . Beginning the defence of their Belgian League title, Racing Genk drew 6–6 with just-promoted Westerlo in a match which also featured five penalties and four red cards.

Ron Eyre scored **two hundred and two** League goals between 1924 and 1933 in a total of 227 games to become Bournemouth's all-time record marksman.

8 August 1981 . . . It wasn't East Stirling's day. The first coach taking them to play Montrose in the League Cup broke down – so did two more. They finally arrived by taxi – and lost 1–0.

9 August 1986 . . . A bad-tempered Scottish Premier Division game between Hibs and Rangers featured a 21-man punch-up which was ignored only by Rangers keeper Alan Rough.

10 August 1974 . . . Kevin Keegan of Liverpool and Billy Bremner of Leeds both lost their shirts on the Charity Shield at Wembley – both ripped off said garments as they were dismissed for fighting.

11 August 1999 . . . The scheduled Worthington Cup match between Torquay and Portsmouth was postponed – because of the total eclipse of the sun. Police said their resources were too stretched to provide cover.

12 August 1967 . . . For several minutes Spurs keeper Pat Jennings was their top scorer for the season, after he scored their first goal in the Charity Shield against Manchester United with a shot from his own area.

13 August 1970 . . . Birth date of England skipper Alan Shearer.

14 August 1880 . . . The first recorded game of soccer in Australia was played at Parramatta Common in Sydney, between the King's School and the Wanderers.

15 August 1981 . . . New Zealand beat Fiji 13–0 in a World Cup qualifier, a record victory.

16 August 1969 . . . The first edition of football magazine *Shoot* hit the streets.

17 August 1988 . . . PSV Eindhoven opened their new stadium with a game against AC Milan.

18 August 1980 . . . The Leicester City FC Stakes made history when two-year-old Spindrifter won, becoming the first horse ridden to 11 consecutive victories in one season by the same jockey – George Duffield.

19 August 1989 . . . Would-be Manchester United chairman Michael Knighton, who attempted to buy the club for £20 million, appeared on the pitch before a home match with Arsenal going through a ball-juggling routine.

20 August 1999 . . . Manchester United striker Dwight Yorke was named Best Dressed Man of the Year by the Menswear Council.

21 August 1965 . . . Keith Peacock came on for Charlton at Bolton in a Second Division game, to become the first sub used in a League match.

22 August 1964 . . . *Match of the Day* received its first outing, on BBC 2, with viewing figures of 750,000.

Ray Crawford's **two hundred and four** League goals and 23 in other competitions, between 1958 and 1969 made him Ipswich Town's all-time leading scorer.

23 August 1997 . . . Paolo di Canio was fined £1,000 for 'hitching up his shorts to spectators' after scoring for Sheffield Wednesday at Wimbledon.

24 August 1967 . . . Birth date of Michael Thomas, who scored a dramatic last-minute winner for Arsenal at Anfield to clinch the First Division championship – and was later transferred to . . . Liverpool.

25 August 1999 . . . Granada TV shelved plans to make a documentary about David Beckham and Victoria Adams when the pair demanded the option to sack staff working on the programme and a fee of £50,000.

26 August 1961 . . . Terry Dyson became the first Spurs player to score a hat-trick against Arsenal as they won 4–3 in Division One.

27 August 1955 . . . Manchester United beat Cuba 3–1 fielding a side with an average age of 22 years 106 days – the youngest ever to represent the club.

28 August 1994 . . . Robbie Fowler scored a hat-trick in just 4 minutes 33 seconds as Liverpool beat Arsenal.

29 August 1942 . . . Rattled by continual barracking from the Crystal Palace supporters during a Football League South fixture, Spurs' Andy Duncan walked off the pitch, never to play for them again.

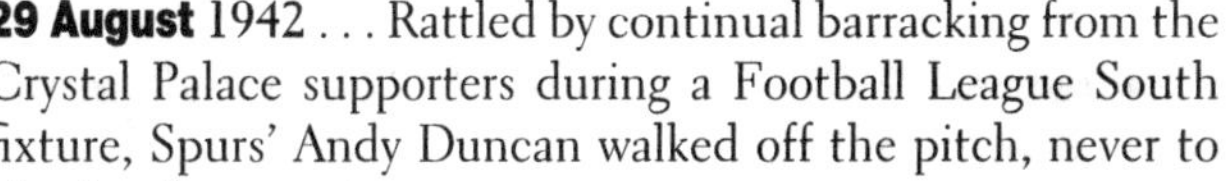

In the spring of 1889, some 10,000 fans paid **two hundred and five** pounds to see non-league Sunderland entertain and wallop double winners Preston North End 4–1.

30 August 1920 . . . Having taken five Surrey wickets for Middlesex at Lord's, keeper Jack Durston raced to play in Brentford's opening home game of the season against Millwall, which they won 1–0.

31 August 1962 . . . After injuring his hand, Reading keeper Arthur Wilkie went up front and scored twice in a 4–2 win over Halifax.

1 September 1952 . . . Scoring his first ever League goal, Aston Villa full-back P. Aldis headed home against Sunderland in Division One – from a reported 35 yards.

2 September 1995 . . . Seventeen people were injured by a single lightning bolt as they sheltered under a tree during a junior football match in Aylesford, Kent. All eventually recovered.

3 September 1930 . . . A record crowd for Newcastle of 68,386 watched the game against Chelsea in Division One.

4 September 1905 . . . Luton entertained Plymouth, who played in green. Kick-off was performed by J.W. Green of brewers J.W. Green Ltd, courtesy of Luton secretary Charles Green, and the referee, Mr Green.

5 September 1987 . . . Chesterfield, the only side in the entire Football League not to have conceded a single goal, went to Gillingham for their sixth Third Division game of the season – and lost 10–0.

6 September 1986 . . . Of 11 First Division matches, eight were away wins, the other three draws.

7 September 1940 . . . The first match to be abandoned due to air raid sirens was at West Ham, where Spurs were winning 4–1 with 80 minutes gone. The result stood.

8 September 1888 . . . The first ever Football League fixtures were played, the five games including a 6–3 win for Derby at Bolton.

9 September 1980 . . . Eammon Collins was just 14 years, 323 days old when he played for Blackpool against Kilmarnock in an Anglo-Scottish Cup game.

10 September 1999 . . . Graham Barber became the first referee to wear a full radio transmission kit giving him two-way communication with his assistants for the Liverpool v Manchester United Premiership match.

11 September 1999 . . . QPR's scheduled First Division game was called off as four players had gone down with suspected meningitis.

12 September 1956 . . . Going directly against the wishes of the Football League, Manchester United beat Anderlecht 2–0 in Brussels to win the first ever European Cup for an English team.

13 September 1968 . . . England international Frank Barson

Aged 44 years, **two hundred and seven** days, Alf Wood became Coventry's oldest player when turning out against Plymouth in the FA Cup.

died – reputedly he served more suspensions than any other player, including nine months of a year-long stint at Watford.

14 September 1996 . . . For the first time in FA Cup history a father and son lined up on opposite sides when 21-year-old Nick Scaife of Bishop Auckland and his dad, Bobby, 41, of Pickering contested a first qualifying round game.

15 September 1982 . . . Paying supporters were banned when Aston Villa beat Besiktas of Turkey 3–1 in a European Cup game, after UEFA disciplinary action.

16 September 1972 . . . With a linesman injured at Highbury where Arsenal were playing Liverpool, Jimmy Hill, there with the *Match of the Day* team, volunteered to run the line.

17 September 1997 . . . Twenty-two penalty shoot-out kicks were taken as Marlow beat Littlehampton 11–10 in an FA Cup first qualifying round second replay which ended when the Littlehampton keeper shot wide.

18 September 1948 . . . Nine Division One matches were drawn – a record for any division of the League on one day.

19 September 1999 . . . Brazilian MP Eurico Miranda, a director of Vasco da Gama, strode on to the pitch to confront referee Paulo Cesar Oliveira, who had just sent off three of his players during a home match with Parana.

20 September 1995 . . . Yorgos Koudas came on for 20

Peter Harris scored **two hundred and eight** League and Cup goals between 1946 and 1960 to become Portsmouth's all-time top scorer.

minutes of the Greece v Yugoslavia match to become the oldest ever international, aged 48 years and 301 days.

21 September 1946 . . . Twins Alfred and William Stephens both scored for Swindon as they beat Exeter 2–0 in the Third Division South.

22 September 1930 . . . Whilst skippering Sheffield in their annual match against Glasgow, J. Seed demanded that the referee should put on a jacket as his white shirt was clashing with those of the Sheffield side.

23 September 1995 . . . For the first time in the Premiership three hat-tricks were scored in one afternoon – by Tony Yeboah for Leeds, Alan Shearer for Blackburn and Robbie Fowler for Liverpool.

24 September 1987 . . . Chelsea chairman Ken Bates was ridiculed when he suggested that football should start its own channel to break the ITV-BBC duopoly on screening matches.

25 September 1982 . . . Reading became the first team to score five in a League (Division Three) match and lose – conceding seven at Doncaster.

26 September 1998 . . . Paolo di Canio of Sheffield Wednesday pushed referee Paul Alcock to the ground after being shown the red card during a game with Arsenal – and later accused the ref of taking a dive.

The Premiership's top tackler for season 1998–99 was Arsenal's Patrick Vieira, winning one hundred and forty-six of a total **two hundred and nine**, a 69.9 per cent success rate.

27 September 1998 . . . Kick-off of the Crystal Palace v Sheffield United match was delayed when a parachutist delivering the match ball fell awkwardly and sustained a suspected broken leg.

28 September 1979 . . . Upset at watching his Tranmere side lose 5–0 at home to Bournemouth, a 72-year-old Rovers fan walloped the Cherries keeper across the backside with a walking stick.

29 September 1951 . . . Making his Crewe debut, keeper Dennis Murray had a nightmare as his side crashed 11–1 to Lincoln.

30 September 1930 . . . The *Manchester Evening News* carried details of the departure of the first Manchester United manager to be sacked – although the paper recorded 'the resignation of Mr James West' and the appointment of Burnley's Ernest Mangnall.

1 October 1938 . . . Fresh from his triumph in assuring the nation that there would be no war, Prime Minister Neville Chamberlain relaxed by watching Everton win the Merseyside derby 2–1.

2 October 1965 . . . Spurs supplied both keepers as Northern Ireland fielded Pat Jennings against Scotland, with Bill Brown in goal.

3 October 1997 . . . UEFA ordered Spartak Moscow to replay their UEFA Cup match against Swiss team Sion because

---

Preston's England winger Tom Finney is the club's all-time leading scorer, with **two hundred and ten** League and FA Cup goals scored between 1946 and 1960.

their goals were found to be 4.7in too low.

4 October 1913 . . . Norman Wood of Stockport scored an own goal, gave away a penalty and missed from the spot as his side lost 3–1 to Fulham.

5 October 1961 . . . Mansfield Town played their first home match under floodlights, against Cardiff.

6 October 1956 . . . Bobby Charlton made his Manchester United debut – against Charlton.

7 October 1946 . . . Albania played their first ever football international – against Yugoslavia, who beat them 3–2.

8 October 1969 . . . Southampton's record crowd of 31,044 watched the game against Manchester United in Division One.

9 October 1961 . . . Gillingham arrived late for their match with Barrow after missing their train – and having finally got there, they lost 7–0.

10 October 1932 . . . An eventful afternoon for Oldham's left-back T. Wynee, who scored against Manchester United with a penalty and a free kick, but also conceded two own goals.

11 October 1995 . . . Duncan Ferguson, Scotland's centre-

Manchester United keeper Jack Crompton played a total of **two hundred and eleven** games for the club – including the 1948 FA Cup final, two days after having an abscess removed from his spine.

forward, became the first professional footballer to be jailed for a violent incident on the pitch, after head-butting a Raith player in April 1994.

12 October 1999 . . . Italy's first match to be officiated by two referees, an Italian Cup match between Sampdoria and Bologna, was abandoned shortly after half-time because of crowd trouble.

13 October 1999 . . . After Scotland and England were paired in the Euro 2000 play-off, England boss Kevin Keegan claimed that he'd had a premonition of the draw when he woke up in his hotel 'hearing bagpipes'.

14 October 1878 . . . Two teams from Sheffield played the first football match under artificial illumination at Bramall Lane, Sheffield, where four lamps were erected on 30ft wooden towers.

15 October 1887 . . . Preston beat Hyde 26–0 in the FA Cup – but the referee reportedly played 30 minutes too much.

16 October 1993 . . . Colchester lost 5–0 at Hereford, in the process becoming the first side ever to have two keepers dismissed during a match.

17 October 1987 . . . Chris Woods, Frank McAvennie and Terry Butcher were all sent off during the 'Old Firm' derby at Ibrox, and later charged with behaviour likely to cause a breach of the peace.

Until a cartilage operation kept him out of their side in 1972, German World Cup star Berti Vogts played **two hundred and twelve** successive League games for Borussia Mönchengladbach.

18 October 1980 . . . A bad day for home sides in Division Two as seven of the ten games were drawn and the three others produced away wins.

19 October 1946 . . . Barnet v Tooting & Mitcham was the first match televised by the BBC following the Second World War.

20 October 1990 . . . Only David Seaman kept his composure as a 21-man brawl broke out during the Manchester United v Arsenal First Division clash at Old Trafford.

21 October 1964 . . . England drew 2–2 with Belgium at Wembley. The shirt worn by Anderlecht defender Georges Heylans was sold at auction in 1998 for £320.

22 October 1988 . . . Brothers Danny, Ray and Rod Wallace all played for Southampton in a First Division game.

23 October 1929 . . . PSV Eindhoven played Amsterdam in a floodlit game, illuminated by lights strung from tram wires around the perimeter of Holland's Olympic Stadium.

24 October 1871 . . . Jules Rimet, who inspired and was immortalised by the World Cup, was born in Thuley, France.

25 October 1924 . . . 2–0 down at Fulham, Stockport County were stunned when the ref blew for time with fully six minutes left – but when he finally restarted the game, two County players had already bathed, dressed and gone home.

Ayr United's leading all-time scorer is Peter Price with **two hundred and thirteen** goals struck between 1955 and 1961.

26 October 1940 . . . Frank Hodgetts became WBA's youngest ever player when he turned out against Notts County, aged 16 years and 26 days.

27 October 1928 . . . Making his debut, Crystal Palace's Wally Betteridge also became their oldest player at 41, in an 8–0 defeat.

28 October 1967 . . . Nottingham Forest set a crowd record of 49,945 against Manchester United in Division One.

29 October 1986 . . . Derby players stopped as they heard a whistle at Aston Villa in their League Cup third round tie. Tony Daley of Villa carried on to score – and the goal stood.

30 October 1960 . . . Diego 'Hand of God' Maradona was born in Buenos Aires.

31 October 1990 . . . Dave Beasant broke a finger playing for Chelsea in a League Cup game with Portsmouth – and his record of 394 consecutive League appearances was over.

1 November 1930 . . . Manchester United beat Birmingham 2–0 at home, having lost their previous 12 matches.

2 November 1999 . . . Thinking the match kicked off at 7.45 p.m., Barnet arrived at Hartlepool at 7.35 p.m., only to discover kick-off was at 7.30 p.m. The club was fined £2,500.

John Robertson is Hearts' leading all-time scorer with **two hundred and fourteen** goals.

3 November 1894 . . . Manchester City lost 5–2 to Newton Heath (later Manchester United) in the first League derby between the two sides.

4 November 1986 . . . Portsmouth's Kevin Dillon scored a penalty hat-trick in a Full Members Cup second round game against Millwall.

5 November 1898 . . . An inside-forward named Cunningham made his debut for Newton Heath. Seventeen games and four months later he was suspended and never played for the club again – he and a prolific scorer named Boyd were kicked out for their off-field boozing activities.

6 November 1991 . . . Both Arsenal (European Cup) and Manchester United (Cup Winners' Cup) were knocked out of Europe.

7 November 1891 . . . The half-time guest of honour at the Rangers v Queen's Park Glasgow Cup quarter-final was western legend Colonel W.F. Cody, alias Buffalo Bill.

8 November 1999 . . . Joan Wayman bought husband John a pair of football boots for his 81st birthday, so that the Watford ref could continue officiating at local league matches.

9 November 1999 . . . With their FA Cup first round replay deadlocked at 1–1 after extra time, Wycombe Wanderers and Oxford City were ready to contest a penalty shoot-out – until an electrical fire broke out, causing an abandonment.

10 November 1997 . . . Bruce Rioch, assistant manager at QPR, discovered he had been dismissed when he saw the news on Ceefax.

11 November 1871 . . . Jarvis Kenrick scored the first FA Cup goal as Clapton won 3–0 at Upton Park.

12 November 1904 . . . Trailing 5–0 to Everton at half-time, Sheffield Wednesday came back to draw 5–5.

13 November 1985 . . . Billy Lane, who scored a hat-trick in three minutes for Watford against Clapton Orient in 1933, died aged 82.

14 November 1934 . . . Arsenal supplied seven of the England team as they played Italy.

15 November 1969 . . . Liverpool beat West Ham 2–0 in the first League match televised in colour by the BBC.

16 November 1991 . . . Tory politician Ken Clarke officially switched on Mansfield Town's new floodlights – only for the match to be abandoned after 32 minutes because of fog.

17 November 1925 . . . Exeter's main stand was destroyed by fire, together with the players' kit – except for Bob Pollard's boots, which had been sent to Northampton for repair.

18 November 1999 . . . Angie Harriott, a cousin of TV chef

Andrew Wilson struck **two hundred and sixteen** League and FA Cup goals between 1900 and 1920 to become Sheffield Wednesday's top scorer.

Ainsley, was officially recognised as the fastest goalscorer in women's football after her seven-second strike for Launton Ladies in the Southern League Premier Division.

19 November 1981 . . . Former England international Malcolm MacDonald became the first paid director of a Football League club when he joined the Fulham board.

20 November 1982 . . . The worst ever day in British football history for sendings-off as 15 players – three in League matches, 12 in FA Cup games, were dismissed.

21 November 1942 . . . Jack Rowley scored all the goals for Wolves in an 8–1 win over Derby.

22 November 1922 . . . W.H. Minter of St Alban's City scored seven times against Dulwich Hamlet in an FA Cup fourth qualifying round replay. They lost 8–7.

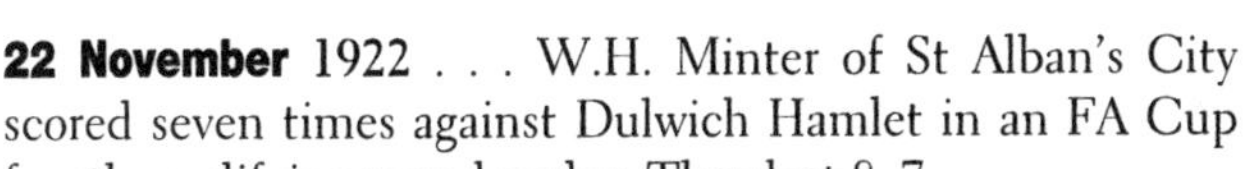

23 November 1946 . . . Jack Balmer scored three goals as Liverpool beat Arsenal 4–2. In his previous game he scored all four as Liverpool won at Derby and in the game before that notched all three against Portsmouth.

24 November 1971 . . . Jim McLean was appointed as manager of Dundee United – and went on to become the first chairman-manager in 1988.

25 November 1425 . . . Professional football was acknowledged for the first time as authorities at Bicester Priory in

An outstanding but controversial striker of the 1950s, Henri Coppens scored a record career total of **two hundred and seventeen** goals in the Belgian League.

Oxfordshire permitted 'gifts to the football players to the sum of fourpence' during the Feast of St Catherine the Martyr.

26 November 1955 . . . Keeper Jack Kelsey had a busy day, playing for Wales in a 2–2 draw at Villa Park against England, then driving himself to Highbury to play for Arsenal as they beat Juventus 3–1.

27 November 1999 . . . Paraguayan keeper Jose Luis Chilavert became the first goalie to score a hat-trick from the penalty spot, for Velez Sarsfield against Ferro Carril in the Argentine League.

28 November 1992 . . . Nottingham Forest had 22 corners to Southampton's two in their Premiership game, but lost 2–1.

29 November 1977 . . . Viv Anderson became the first black player to represent England in a full international.

30 November 1999 . . . Manchester United became the first English side to win the World Club Championship when they beat Palmeiras of Brazil 1–0 in Tokyo.

1 December 1999 . . . The Professional Footballers' Association paid £1.9 million for the painting 'Going To The Match' by L.S. Lowry – completed in 1953 and based on his memories of Bolton Wanderers' Burnden Park ground.

2 December 1997 . . . Four Bristol Rovers players and one from Wigan were dismissed in their Second Division game.

Lindsay Smith, aged 16 years, **two hundred and eighteen** days, became Colchester's youngest player in a League match against Grimsby in April 1971.

3 December 1994 . . . 'Spurs or Bye will play Altrincham' – the unusual FA Cup third round draw, made when Spurs were appealing against a decision to ban them from the competition.

4 December 1935 . . . England beat Germany 3–0 at White Hart Lane. Arsenal defender George Male played and in 1998 the shirt he wore and cap he won were sold at auction for £700 and £880 respectively.

5 December 1931 . . . The 0–0 draw between Newcastle and Portsmouth in Division One produced not a single corner.

6 December 1930 . . . The lowest League gate for a Saturday afternoon was recorded when just 469 turned up to see Thames beat Luton 1–0 in the Third Division South.

7 December 1990 . . . Scarborough attracted a crowd of just 625 for their Fourth Division game with Wrexham.

8 December 1984 . . . Nine players scored as Stirling Albion beat Selkirk 20–0 in the first round of the Scottish Cup.

9 December 1990 . . . Giuseppe Lorenzo of Bologna was sent off after ten seconds for striking a member of the Parma side.

10 December 1985 . . . The Isles of Scilly League, the smallest in the world, announced a sponsorship deal by a local double glazing company. The League boasted two teams, playing each other every week.

Aged 43 years, **two hundred and nineteen** days, Mick Burns turned out against Gateshead in a January 1952 game to become Ipswich's oldest ever player.

11 December 1990 . . . Neil Webb became the first England 'B' player sent off, during an away game against Algeria.

12 December 1891 . . . Playing in a blizzard, Burnley were 3–0 up against Blackburn when both captains were sent off for fighting.

13 December 1942 . . . Stefan Stanis of Racing Club Lens scored 16 goals as his side beat Aubry-Asturies 32–0.

14 December 1935 . . . Ted Drake hit seven as Arsenal won at Aston Villa.

15 December 1999 . . . Former German international keeper Harald Schumacher was sacked as boss of Fortuna Cologne – at half-time of their match against Waldhof Mannheim.

16 December 1972 . . . Manchester United lost 5–0 to bottom-of-the-table Crystal Palace.

17 December 1955 . . . Arsenal full-back D. Evans heard ref F.B. Coultas blow for time and promptly whacked the ball into his own net. Sadly for him it had been a spectator's whistle and an own goal was awarded.

18 December 1954 . . . Perhaps uniquely, Leicester's Stan Milburn and Jack Froggatt were credited with a joint own goal against Chelsea.

---

19 December 1990 . . . Matthias Sammer, 23, was the first East German picked for the new united German side as they played Switzerland in Stuttgart.

20 December 1983 . . . The original World Cup, the Jules Rimet trophy, was stolen from the Brazilian FA's offices and never recovered.

21 December 1894 . . . Division Two side Walsall Swifts went on strike for 20 minutes before their home game against Newcastle was due to kick off, arguing over financial incentives.

22 December 1967 . . . Birth date of one of the few players named after a television programme – Dan Petrescu.

23 December 1959 . . . Capital Radio and Channel 5 TV commentator Jonathan Pearce, he of the excitable vocal style, was born in Plymouth.

24 December 1881 . . . Having lost 6–2 to Dumbarton in the Scottish Cup round five, Hibs protested on the grounds of an ineligible player and were awarded a replay. The result – 6–2 to Dumbarton.

25 December 1891 . . . Darwen fans rioted before a friendly against Blackburn Rovers – breaking the goalposts, smashing dressing room windows and ripping up carpets in the stand.

26 December 1935 . . . Robert 'Bunny' Bell missed a penalty

for Tranmere in their 13–4 win over Oldham – but he did score nine other goals.

27 December 1938 . . . W. Cook scored from the spot for Everton against Derby in Division One – having done the same the day before, also against Derby, and on 24 December against Blackpool.

28 December 1993 . . . For the first time all four permitted subs scored as Barnet beat Torquay 5–4.

29 December 1906 . . . Birmingham's Benny Green scored the club's first ever goal at St Andrew's in a 3–0 win over Preston – and was rewarded by the gift of a piano.

30 December 1999 . . . Former Manchester United and Danish international keeper Peter Schmeichel announced that he had bought Danish Premier League side Hvidovre.

31 December 1906 . . . The day on which the suspension of Billy Meredith ended. In August 1905 the Manchester City star was banned for allegedly bribing an Aston Villa player. While suspended he was signed by Manchester United.

Aged 37 years, **two hundred and twenty-two** days, Lawrie Madden became Wolves' oldest player in May 1993.

Sweden's Euro 2000 star Freddie Ljungberg claimed that he wasn't bothered by his country's 'no sex before matches' decree – 'if anyone offers me sex the night before a match I always say "No thanks" because I want to keep the feeling in my feet. It sort of disappears if you have sex before a match.'

Police arrested a Dutch fan for painting his rented house orange.

England's official suits for the tournament were grey, by Burton, and modelled on the 1966 World Cup model.

Recruited as a TV pundit, John Barnes, famous for his flamboyant fashion sense was warned by ITV chiefs to tone down the suits to avoid causing optical illusions and strobing of TV pictures.

Thirty-year-old Yugoslav defender Nisa Saveljic was released

Bobby Charlton notched **two hundred and twenty-three** goals in 708 Manchester United senior appearances.

by Belgrade police after being arrested for failing to perform obligatory military service.

Dutch midfielder Edgar Davids became the world's largest ever building wrap project when his 150 metre high image, the same size as the Statue of Liberty, was wrapped around the Rotterdam HQ of the Nationale-Nederland insurance company.

The Thai army forbade squaddies from betting on Euro 2000 incase problems arose when they lost their salaries.

After England's opening game had passed off in a comparatively trouble-free manner – although David Beckham gave a one-fingered salute to 'fans' who abused him and other players following their defeat by Portugal – Dutch police offered an interesting theory why: 'Cannabis may have helped relax them' said Eindhoven police chief Johann Beelan.

The Commission for Racial Equality in Wales condemned a Swansea publican for offering free beer every time a goal was scored against England.

talkSPORT radio station was humiliated when forced in the High Court to admit that its 'live coverage' of Euro 2000 games was actually being broadcast from a studio in Amsterdam where presenters were watching TV and sound effects were added to their 'commentaries'.

Football fans Rick Thomas, 33, and Trevor Cole, 37, from

Sunderland's Charles Buchan scored **two hundred and twenty-four** goals in 413 League and Cup appearances for them up to 1925.

Bristol locked themselves in a 14 x 8ft garden shed for the duration of the tournament to watch every match.

Some names which caused commentators to pause – Germany's Butt, Ballack and Jancker; Belgium's Goor; Italy's Totti; Czech Fukal and Dutchmen Cocu and Conterman.

Clapham chippie Ben Stylianou helped England fans find cod – by using food dye to serve up fish with a red cross of St. George on.

During Euro 2000, prostitutes in The Hague applied unsuccessfully to the Mayor for an extension to their working hours because business had collapsed due to punters watching the football.

Born in Rotterdam, with a Belgian father and Dutch mother, living in Belgium, Raymond Brul painted half of his car in Dutch colours, the other half in Belgian.

A Dutch waste disposal company coloured a football pitch orange and put 22 cows, each with a number on them into it, while a farmer in the Dutch town of Clinge dressed his sheep in orange wizard hats.

Yugoslav fans Bojan Gilgoraic, 24, and Milorad Majkic, 53, cycled 995 miles in ten days to get to the tournament.

Public urinals in some parts of Holland were provided with miniature goals for (male) patrons to aim through.

On 24 August, 1972, Brian Clough paid a record British fee of **two hundred and twenty-five** thousand pounds to bring Leicester defender David Nish to Derby.

Germany's striker Paolo Rink went to collect a ball he'd kicked out of their training ground only to see a young lady pedalling off with it on a bicycle.

'I love the sensuality and sexuality that emanates from leather – it multiplies one's sensations tenfold' Emmanuel Petit told France Soir during Euro 2000.

Turkish midfielder Tugay Kerimoglu was sent home by coach Mustafa Denzli afters throwing a water bottle, or shinpads, depending on which version you believe, at him after being substituted.

Edgar Davids, who has to wear glasses during matches because of a medical condition was given special dispensation to use an eyewash which could make him fail a drugs test. He donated his £100,000 glasses endorsement fee towards research into the condition.

Following the German's exit, phone giant Deutsche Telekom, which had been running TV ads showing players using their mobiles withdrew them for fear 'that they may damage the image of the product'.

An Amsterdam sex shop selling orange vibrators was refused permission by Euro 2000 organisers to add the official logo to them.

A topless nightclub revue in Bangkok featuring dancing girls with Euro 2000 teams names written on their chests in whipped cream was threatened with closure by the vice squad.

Gianfranco Zola played two thousand **two hundred and twenty-six** minutes for Chelsea during Premiership season 1999/2000.

It was revealed that the Romanian team sponsor a monastery.

After Raul hoisted his last minute penalty against France in the Quarter Final over the bar, Youri Djorkaeff, French midfielder, took the credit: 'I used voodoo. I put the Indian sign on the kick' he claimed after being seen to sprinkle grass on the ball and cross himself – reminiscent of Uri Geller's claim to have moved the ball when Gary McAllister took a Euro 96 penalty for Scotland against England and missed.

French star Dugarry played much of the Quarter Final against Spain sporting cotton wool shoved up both nostrils in an effort to halt bleeding.

'The way Italy play reminds me of one of those mothers who prefer their kids to rot away their youth inside the family homes: outside as everybody knows there is a violent world of temptations, not to mention flower pots poised to fall off balconies on to their heads' – former Argentina striker Jorge Valdano's comment about Italy's Euro 2000 displays.

Virgin Atlantic claimed a football first by screening Euro 2000 matches on inflight entertainment systems on longhaul routes the day after games were played.

Journalist Trevor Haylett was hired by UEFA to write an article about England's performances for the tournament media information service. So critical were his comments that he was dismissed.

Liverpool were one of the hottest favourites to win the FA Cup Final in 1987/88, but the (2/7) favourites were shock 1–0 losers to Wimbledon.

French defender Desailly revealed that his real passion in life is making chocolate souffles.

'**I** do have a small problem with my eyes. I sometimes lose sight of things but it is not a big problem' said Spanish striker Raul who missed a vital last minute penalty against France.

Dugarry came out for the 2nd half of the Final with cotton wool buds up each nostril after taking the ball full in the face at the end of the first half. After checking he wasn't leaking in a sanguinary manner he discarded them

Euro 2000 referee was the first in a major final named after a Grand National winner – Mr Frisk.

BIBLIOGRAPHY

Appleton, Arthur, *Hotbed of Soccer* (Sportsmans Book Club 1961)

Australian Society for Sports History, *The Oxford Companion to Australian Sport* (Oxford 1992)

Barnett, Neil, *Official Chelsea FC Fact File* (Boxtree 1998)

Barrett, Norman, *Daily Telegraph Football Chronicle* (Ebury Press 1996)

Barrett, Norman, *World Soccer from A to Z* (Book Club Associates 1973)

Betts, Graham, *Spurs* (Mainstream 1998)

Betts, Graham, *The Villains* (Mainstream 1998)

Betts, Graham, *United* (Mainstream 1998)

Butler, Bryon, *100 Seasons of League Football* (Lennard Queen Anne Press 1998)

Collett, Mike, *The Guinness Record of the FA Cup* (Guinness 1993)

Delaney, Terence, *The Footballer's Bedside Book* (SBC 1963)

Drewett, Jim and Leith, Alex, *The Virgin Football Records* (Virgin 1997)

Edelston, Maurice and Delaney, Terence, *Masters of Soccer* (SBC 1962)

Engel, Matthew and Morrison, Ian, *Sportspages Almanac 1991, 1992* (Sports pages)

Freddi, Chris, *Guinness Sports Yearbook 1995* (Guinness)

Golesworthy, Maurice, *Encyclopaedia of Association Football* (Robert Hale 1965)

Glanvill, Rick, *Chelsea Who's Who* (Boxtree 1998)

Glanville, Brian, *The Story of the World Cup* (Faber and Faber 1997)

Hayes, Dean, *Burnley FC Complete A to Z* (Sigma 1999)

Hayes, Dean, *Goodison Park Encyclopaedia* (Mainstream 1998)

Hayes, Dean, *Stockport County FC, A-Z* (Sigma 1998)

Hayes, Dean, *The Molineux Encyclopaedia* (Mainstream 1999)
Hayes, Dean, *The St Andrew's Encyclopaedia* (Mainstream 1999)
Hayes, Dean, *Tranmere Rovers: Complete A to Z* (Sigma 1999)
Holland, Julian, *Spurs* (SBC 1957)
Hulme, David, *Best Book of Football Songs and Chants Ever!* (Carlton 1998)
Hugman, Barry J., *1998–99 Official FA Footballers Factfile* (Lennard Queen Anne Press)
James, Brian, *England v Scotland* (SBC 1970)
Jeffery, Gordon, *European International Football* (SBC 1965)
Joy, Bernard, *European International Football* (SBC 1965)
Lerman, Richard and Brown, David, *The Reds* (Mainstream 1998)
Lerman, Richard and Brown, David, *The Blues* (Mainstream 1998)
Lowndes, William, *The Story of Football* (SBC 1964)
Miller, Clark, *He Always Puts it to the Right* (Victor Gollancz 1998)
Moore, Steve, *Fortean Times Book of Weird Sex* (John Brown 1995)
Nawrat, Chris, Hutchings, Steve and Struthers, Greg, *Sunday Times Chronicle of Twentieth Century Sport* (W.H. Smith 1992)
Nichols, Peter, *BBC Radio 5 Live Sports Yearbook 1995, 96, 97, 98, 99* (Oddball)
Nichols, Peter, *Guinness Sports Yearbook 1994* (Guinness)
Radnege, Kier, *Complete Encyclopaedia of Football* (Carlton 1998)
Rollin, Jack, *Soccer at War 1939–45* (Collins Willow 1985)
Rollin, Jack and Barrett, Norman, *Telegraph Football Yearbook 86–87* (Telegraph)
Signy, Dennis, *A Pictorial History of Soccer* (Hamlyn 1968)
Tatham, Dick, *Football Champions* (Purnell 1964)
Tibballs, Geoff, *Great Sporting Failures* (Collins Willow 1993)
Topical Times Football Book (D. C. Thomson 1961–2, 1962–3)
Tyler, Martin, *Cup Final Extra!* (Hamlyn 1981)

Wallechinsky, David, *The Complete Book of the Olympics* (Aurum 1996)

White, John, *Manchester United Book of Lists* (MUB 1999)

Willmore, G.A., *West Bromwich Albion: The First Hundred Years* (Readers Union 1980)

Young, Percy M., *A History of British Football* (Stanley Paul 1968)